TEN

Short Stories

BLOOMSBURY
CLASSICS

'She Wasn't Soft ' by T. Coraghessan Boyle first appeared in the *New Yorker*, September 1995; 'The Drowned Son' by David Guterson first appeared in *Harper's Magazine*, February 1996; 'Maître Mussard's Bequest' by Patrick Süskind first appeared as 'Das Vermächtnis des Maître Mussard' (1975) in Neue Deutsche Hefte, No. 149, Berlin 1976, copyright © Patrick Süskind and © Diogenes Verlag AG Zurich for this edition, translation © 1995 by Irving Wardle; 'Two Boys and a Girl' by Tobias Wolff first appeared in *Antaeus*, 1995.

Bloomsbury Publishing Plc,
2 Soho Square, London W1V 6HB

A CIP catalogue record for this book
is available from the British Library

ISBN 0 7475 2916 7

10 9 8 7 6 5 4 3 2 1

Typeset by Hewer Text Composition Services, Edinburgh
Printed by St Edmundsbury Press, Suffolk
Jacket design by Jeff Fisher

Contents

The Labrador Fiasco
Margaret Atwood

It's October; but which October? One of those Octobers, with their quick intensities of light, their diminuendos, their red and orange leaves. My father is sitting in his armchair by the fire. He has on his black and white checked dressing gown, over his other clothes, and his old leather slippers, with his feet propped up on a hassock. Therefore it must be evening.

My mother is reading to him. She fiddles with her glasses, and hunches over the page; or it looks like hunching. In fact that is just the shape she is now.

My father is grinning, so this must be a part he enjoys. His grin is higher on the left side than on the right: six years ago he had a stroke, which we all pretend he's recovered from; and he has, mostly.

'What's happening now?' I say, taking off my coat. I already know the story, having heard it before.

'They've just set out,' says my mother.

My father says, 'They took the wrong supplies.' This pleases him: he himself would not have taken the wrong supplies. In fact he would never have gone on this ill-advised journey in the first place, or – although he was once more reckless, more impetuous, more sure of his ability to confront fate and transcend danger – this is his opinion now. 'Darn fools,' he says, grinning away.

But what supplies could they have taken, other than the wrong ones? White sugar, white flour, rice; that was what you took then. Peameal, sulphured apples, hard-tack, bacon, lard. Heavy things. There was no freeze-drying then, no handy packaged soups; there were no nylon vests, no pocket-sized sleeping bags, no light-weight tarpaulins. Their tent was made of balloon silk, oiled to waterproof it. Their blankets were of wool. The packsacks were canvas, with leather straps and tump-lines that went across the forehead to cut the strain on the back. They would have smelled of tar. In addition there were two rifles, two pistols, 1,200 rounds of ammunition, a camera and a sextant; and then the cooking utensils and the clothing. Every pound of it had to be carried over each and every portage, or hauled upriver in the canoe, which was eighteen feet long, wood-framed and canvas-covered.

None of this would have daunted the adventurers, however; or not at first. There were two of them, two young Americans; they'd been on camping expeditions before, although at warmer latitudes, with fragrant evening pipes smoked before cheerful blazes and a fresh-caught trout sizzling in the pan while the sunsets paled in the west. Each would have been able to turn a neat, Kiplingesque paragraph or two on the lure of wild places, the challenge of the unknown. This was in 1903, when exploration was still in vogue as a test of manliness, and when manliness itself was still in vogue, and was thought to couple naturally with the word 'clean'. Manliness, cleanliness, the wilderness, where you could feel free. With gun and fishing rod, of course. You could live off the land.

The leader of the expedition, whose name was Hubbard, worked for a magazine dedicated to the outdoors. His idea was that he and his chum and cousin – whose name was Wallace – would penetrate the last unmapped Labrador wilds, and he would write a series of articles about their adventures, and thus make his name. (These were his very words: 'I will make my name.') Specifically, they would ascend the Nascaupee River, said to flow out of Lake Michikamau, a fabled inland lake teeming with fish; from there they could make it to the George River, where the Indians congregated every summer for the caribou hunt, and from there to a Hudson's Bay post, and out to the coast again. While among the Indians, Hubbard planned to do a little amateur anthropology, which he would also write up, with photographs – a shaggy-haired hunter with an old-fashioned rifle, his foot on a carcass; a cut-off head, with spreading antlers. Women with bead necklaces and gleaming eyes chewing the hide, or sewing it, or whatever they did. *The Last Wild People.* Something like that. There was a great interest in such subjects. He would describe the menus, too.

(But those Indians came from the north. No one ever took the river route from the west and south.)

In stories like this, there is always – there is supposed to be – an old Indian who appears to the white men as they are planning to set out. He comes to warn them, because he is kind at heart and they are ignorant. 'Do not go there,' he says. 'That is a place we never go.' Indians in these tales have a formal manner of speaking.

'Why not?' the white men say.

'Bad spirits live there,' says the old Indian. The white men smile and thank him, and disregard his advice. Native superstition, they think. So they go where they've been warned not to, and then, after many hardships, they die. The old Indian shakes his head when he hears of it. Foolish white men, but what can you tell them? They have no respect.

There's no old Indian in this book – he somehow got
left out – so my father takes the part upon himself. 'They
shouldn't have gone there,' he says. 'The Indians never
went that way.' He doesn't say *bad spirits*, however. He
says, 'Nothing to eat.' For the Indians it would have been
the same thing, because where does food come from if
not from the spirits? It isn't just there, it is given; or else
withheld.

Hubbard and Wallace tried to hire several Indians, to
come with them at least on the first stages of the journey,
and to help with the packs. None would go; they said
they were 'too busy'. Really they knew too much. What
they knew was that you couldn't possibly carry with you,
in there, everything you would need to eat. And if you
couldn't carry it you would have to kill it. But most of the
time there was nothing to kill. 'Too busy' meant too busy
to die. It also meant too polite to point out the obvious.

The two explorers did do one thing right. They hired a
guide. His name was George, and he was a Cree Indian, or
partly; what they called then a 'breed'. He was from James
Bay, too far away from Labrador to know the full and evil
truth about it. George travelled south to meet his employ-
ers, all the way to New York City, where he had never
been before. He had never been to the United States
before, or even to a city. He kept calm, he looked about
him; he demonstrated his resourcefulness by figuring out
what a taxi-cab was and how to hire one. His ability to
reason things through was to come in very handy later on.

'That George was quite a boy,' says my father. George
is his favourite person in the whole story.

Somewhere around the house there's a picture of my
father himself – at the back of a photo album, perhaps, with
the snapshots that haven't yet been stuck in. It shows him
thirty years younger, on some canoe trip or another – if you

don't write these things down on the backs of the pictures,
they get forgotten. He's evidently crossing a portage. He
hasn't shaved, he's got a bandanna tied around his head
because of the blackflies and mosquitoes, and he's carrying
a heavy pack, with the broad tump-line across his forehead.
His hair is dark, his glistening face is deeply tanned and not
what you'd call clean. He looks slightly villainous; like a
pirate, or indeed like a northwoods guide, the kind that
might suddenly vanish in the middle of the night, along
with your best rifle, just before the wolves arrive on the
scene. But like someone who knows what he's doing.

'That George knew what he was doing,' says my
father now.

Once he got out of New York, that is; while there,
George wasn't much help, because he didn't know where
to shop. It was in New York that the two men bought all
the necessary supplies, except a gill net, which they thought
they could find up north. They also failed to purchase extra
moccasins. This may have been their worst mistake.

Then they set out, by train and then by boat and then
by smaller boat. The details are tedious. The weather was
bad, the meals were foul, none of the transportation was
ever on time. They spent a lot of hours and even days
waiting around on docks and wondering when their
luggage would turn up.

'That's enough for tonight,' says my mother.

'I think he's asleep,' I say.

'He never used to go to sleep,' says my mother. 'Not
with this story. Usually he's busy making up his list.'

'His list?'

'His list of what he would take.'

While my father sleeps, I skip ahead in the story. The
three men have finally made it inland from the bleak

north-eastern shore of Labrador, and have left their last
jumping-off place, and are voyaging in earnest. It's the
middle of July, but the short summer will soon be over,
and they have five hundred miles to go.

Their task is to navigate Grand Lake, which is long
and thin; at its extreme end, or so they've been told, the
Nascaupee flows into it. The only map they've seen,
crudely drawn by an earlier white traveller some fifty
years before, shows Grand Lake with only one river
emptying into it. One is all the Indians have ever
mentioned: the one that goes somewhere. Why talk
about the others, because why would anyone want to
know about them? There are many plants which have no
names because they cannot be eaten or used.

But in fact there are four other rivers.

During this first morning they are exhilarated, or so
Wallace records. Their hopes are high, adventure calls.
The sky is deep blue, the air is crisp, the sun is bright,
the treetops seem to beckon them on. They do not
know enough to beware of beckoning treetops. For
lunch they have flapjacks and syrup, and are filled with
a sense of well-being. They know they're going into
danger, but they also know that they are immortal.
Such moods do occur, in the north. They take pictures
with their camera: of their laden canoe, of one
another: moustached, be-sweatered, with puttee-
shaped wrappings on their legs and things on their
heads that look like bowler hats, leaning blithely on
their paddles. Heartbreaking, but only when you
know the end. As it is they're having the time of
their lives.

There's another photo of my father, perhaps from the
same trip as the one with the portage; or he's wearing the
same bandanna. This time he's grinning into the camera

lens, pretending to shave himself with his axe. Two tall-
tale points are being made: that his axe is as sharp as a
razor, and that his bristles are so tough that only an axe
could cut them. It's highjinks, a canoe-trip joke;
although secretly of course he once believed both of
these things.

On the second day the three men pass the mouth of
the Nascaupee, which is hidden behind an island and
looks like shoreline. They don't even suspect it is
there. They continue on to the end of the lake, and
enter the river they find there. They've taken the
wrong turn.

I don't get back to Labrador for over a week. When I
return, it's a Sunday night. The fire is blazing away and
my father is sitting in front of it, waiting to see what will
happen next. My mother is rustling up the baking-
powder biscuits and the decaffeinated tea. I forage for
cookies.

'How is everything?' I say.

'Fine,' she says. 'But he doesn't get enough exercise.'
Everything means my father, as far as she is concerned.

'You should make him go for a walk,' I say.

'*Make* him,' she says.

'Well, suggest.'

'He doesn't see the point of walking just to walk,' she
says. 'If you're not going anywhere.'

'You could send him on errands,' I say. To this she
does not bother even to reply.

'He says his feet hurt,' she says. I think of the array of
almost-new boots and shoes in the cupboard; boots and
shoes that have proliferated lately. He keeps buying other
ones. If only he can find the right pair, he must think,
whatever it is that's causing his feet to hurt will go away.

I carry in the teacups, dole out the plates. 'So, how are Hubbard and Wallace coming along?' I say. 'Have you got to the place where they eat the owl?'

'Slim pickings,' he says. 'They took the wrong river. Even if they'd found the right one, it was too late to start.'

Hubbard and Wallace and George toil upstream. The heat at midday is oppressive. Flies torment them, little flies like pinpricks, giant ones as big as your thumb. The river is barely navigable: they have to haul their laden canoe over gravel shallows, or portage around rapids, through forest that is harsh and unmarked and jumbled. In front of them the river unrolls; behind them it closes up like a maze. The banks of the river grow steeper; hill after hill, gentle in outline, hard at the core. It's a sparse landscape: ragged spruce, birch, aspen, all spindly; in some places burned over, the way forward blocked by charred and fallen treetrunks.

How long is it before they realise they've gone up the wrong river? Far too long. They cache some of their food so they won't have to carry it; they throw some of it away. They manage to shoot a caribou, which they eat, leaving the hooves and head behind. Their feet hurt; their moccasins are wearing out.

At last Hubbard climbs a high hill, and from its top he sees Lake Michikamau; but the river they have been following does not go there. The lake is too far away: they can't possibly haul their canoe that far through the forest. They will have to turn back.

In the evenings their talk is no longer of discovery and exploration. Instead they talk about what they will eat. What they'll eat tomorrow, and what they'll eat when

they get back. They compose bills of fare, feasts, grand
blowouts. George is able to shoot or catch this and that.
A duck here, a grouse there. A whiskeyjack. They catch
sixty trout, painstakingly one by one, using a hook and
line because they have no gill net. The trout are clear and
fresh as icewater, but only six inches long. Nothing is
nearly enough. The work of travelling uses up more
energy than they can take in; they are slowly dissolving,
wasting away.

Meanwhile the nights become longer and longer and
darker and darker. Ice forms on the edges of the river.
Hauling the canoe over the shallows, through the
rushing stone-cold water, leaves them shivering and
gasping. The first snowflurries fall.

'It's rough country,' says my father. 'No moose; not
even bears. That's always a bad sign, no bears.' He's been
there, or near it; same sort of terrain. He speaks of it with
admiration and nostalgia, and a kind of ruefulness. 'Now
of course you can fly in. You can cover their whole
route in a couple of hours.' He waves his fingers
dismissively: so much for planes.

'What about the owl?' I say.

'What owl?' says my father.

'The one they ate,' I say. 'I think it's where the canoe
dumps, and they save their matches by sticking them in
their ears.'

'I think that was the others,' says my father. 'The ones
who tried the same thing later. I don't think this bunch
ate an owl.'

'If they had eaten one, what sort of owl would it have
been?' I say.

'Great Horned or Boreal,' he says, 'if they were lucky.
More meat on those. But it may have been something
smaller.' He gives a series of thin, eerie barks, like a dog at

a distance, and then he grins. He knows every bird up there by its call; he still does.

'He's sleeping too much in the afternoons,' says my mother.

'Maybe he's tired,' I say.

'He shouldn't be that tired,' she says. 'Tired, and restless as well. He's losing his appetite.'

'Maybe he needs a hobby,' I say. 'Something to occupy his mind.'

'He used to have a lot of them,' my mother says.

I wonder where they've all gone, those hobbies. Their tools and materials are still around; the plane and the spirit level, the feathers for tying dry flies, the machine for enlarging prints, the points for making arrows. These bits and pieces seem to me like artefacts, the kind that are dug up at archaeological sites, and then pondered over and classified, and used for deducing the kind of life once lived.

'He used to say he wanted to write his memoirs,' says my mother. 'A sort of account; all the places he's been. He did begin it several times, but now he's lost interest. He can't see too well.'

'He could use a tape recorder,' I say.

'Oh help,' says my mother. 'More gadgets!'

The winds howl and cease, the snow falls and stops falling. The three men have traversed across to a different river, hoping it will be better, but it isn't. One night George has a dream: God appears to him, shining and bright and affable, and speaks in a manner which is friendly but firm. 'I can't spare any more of these trout,' he says, 'but if you stick to this river you'll get down to Grand Lake all right. Just you don't leave the river, and I'll get you out safe.'

George tells the others of his dream. It is discounted. The men abandon their canoe and strike out overland, hoping to reach their old trail. After far too long they do reach it, and stumble along it down the valley of the river they first ascended, rummaging through their former campsites for any food they might have thrown away. They aren't counting in miles, but in days; how many days they have left, and how many it will take. But that will depend on the weather, and on their own strength: how fast they can go. They find a lump of mouldering flour, a bit of lard, a few bones, some caribou hooves, which they boil. A little tin of dry mustard; they mix it into the soup, and find it encouraging.

In the third week of October, this is how things stand:

Hubbard has become too weak to go any further. He's been left behind, wrapped in his blankets, in the tent, with a fire going. The other two have gone on; they hope to walk out, then send help back for him. He's given them the last of the peameal.

The snow is falling. For dinner he has some strong tea and bone broth, and some boiled rawhide, made from the last of his moccasins; he writes in his journal that it is truly delicious. Now he is without footgear. He has every hope that the others will succeed, and will return and save him; or so he records. Nevertheless he begins a farewell message for his wife. He writes that he has a pair of cowhide mittens which he is looking forward to cooking and eating the next day.

After that he goes to sleep, and after that he dies.

Some days further down the trail, Wallace too has to give up. He and George part company: Wallace intends to go back with the latest leavings they've managed to locate – a few handfuls of mouldy flour. He will find

Hubbard, and together they will await rescue. But
he's been caught in a blizzard, and has lost his
bearings; at the moment he's in a shelter made of
branches, waiting for the snow to let up. He is
amazingly weak, and no longer hungry, which he
knows is a bad sign. Every movement he makes is
slow and deliberate, and at the same time unreal, as if
his body is apart from him and he is only watching it.
In the white light of day or the red flicker of the fire
– for he still has fire – the patterns on the ends of his
own fingers appear miraculous to him. Such clarity
and detail; he follows the pattern of the woven
blanket as if tracing a map.

His dead wife has appeared to him, and has given him
several pieces of practical advice concerning his sleeping
arrangements: a thicker layer of spruce boughs under-
neath, she's said, would be more comfortable. Sometimes he only hears her, sometimes he sees her as well;
she's wearing a blue summer dress, her long hair pinned
up in a shining coil. She appears perfectly at home; the
poles of the shelter are visible through her back. Wallace
has ceased to be surprised by this.

Even further along, George continues to walk; to
walk out. He knows more or less where he's going; he
will find help and return with it. But he isn't out yet,
he's still in. Snow surrounds him, the blank grey sky
enfolds him; at one point he comes across his own
tracks and realises he's been walking in a circle. He too
is thin and weak, but he's managed to shoot a
porcupine. He pauses to think it through: he could
turn around, retrace his steps, take the porcupine back
to share with the others; or he could eat all of it
himself, and go forward. He knows that if he goes
back it's likely that none of them will get out alive; but

if he goes on, there's at least a possibility, at least for him. He goes on, hoarding the bones.

'That George did the right thing,' says my father.

While sitting at the dinner table my father has another stroke. This time it knocks out half the vision in each eye, and his short-term memory, and his sense of where he is. From one minute to the next he has become lost; he gropes through the living room as if he's never been in such a place before. The doctors say this time it's unlikely he'll recover.

Time passes. Now the lilacs are in bloom outside the window, and he can see them, or parts of them. Despite this he thinks it's October. Still, the core of him is still there. He sits in his armchair, trying to figure things out. One sofa cushion looks much like another unless you have something to go by. He watches the sunlight gleaming on the hardwood floor; his best guess is it's a stream. In extreme situations you have to use your wits.

'I'm here,' I say, kissing his dry cheek. He hasn't gone bald, not in the least. He has silvery-white hair, like an egret frozen.

He peers at me, out of the left sides of his eyes, which are the ones that work. 'You seem to have become very old all of a sudden,' he says.

As far as we can tell he's missing the last four or five years, and several blocks of time before that as well. He's disappointed in me: not because of anything I've done, but because of what I've failed to do. I've failed to remain young. If I could have managed that I could have saved him; then he too could have remained as he was.

I wish I could think of something to amuse him. I've tried recordings of bird songs, but he doesn't like them: they remind him that there's something he once knew,

but can't remember. Stories are no good, not even short
ones, because by the time you get to the second page he's
forgotten the beginning. Where are we without our
plots?

Music is better; it takes place drop by drop.

My mother doesn't know what to do, and so she
rearranges: cups and plates, documents, bureau drawers.
Right now she's outside, yanking weeds out of the
garden in a bewildered frenzy. Dirt and couch grass fly
through the air: that at least will get done! There's a
wind; her hair is wild, blown up around her head like
feathers.

I've told her I can't stay long. 'You can't?' she said.
'But we could have tea, I could light a fire . . .'

'Not today,' I said firmly.

He can see her out there, more or less, and he wants
her to come back in. He doesn't like it that she's on the
other side of the glass. If he lets her slip away, out of his
sight, who knows where she might go? She might vanish
for ever.

I hold his good hand. 'She'll come in soon,' I say; but
soon could be a year.

'I want to go home,' he says. I know there's no point
telling him that home is where he now is, because he
means something else. He means the way he was before.

'Where are we now?' I say.

He gives me a crafty look: am I trying to trip him up?
'In a forest,' he says. 'We need to get back.'

'We're all right here,' I say.

He considers. 'Not much to eat.'

'We brought the right supplies,' I say.

He is reassured. 'But there's not enough wood.' He's
anxious about this; he says it every day. His feet are cold,
he says.

'We can get more wood,' I say. 'We can cut it.'

He's not so sure. 'I never thought this would happen,' he says. He doesn't mean the stroke, because he doesn't know he's had one. He means getting lost.

'We know what to do,' I say. 'Anyway, we'll be fine.'

'We'll be fine,' he says, but he sounds dubious. He doesn't trust me, and he is right.

The story related within this story may be found in its original version in The Lure of the Labrador Wild, *by Dillon Wallace, published in 1905 by Fleming H. Revell Company, and reprinted by Breakwater Books, Newfoundland, in 1977.*

She Wasn't Soft
T. Coraghessan Boyle

She wasn't tender, she wasn't soft, she wasn't sweetly yielding or coquettish, and she was nobody's little woman and never would be. That had been her mother's role, and look at the sad sack of neuroses and alcoholic dysfunction *she'd* become. And her father. He'd been the pasha of the living room, the sultan of the kitchen, and the emperor of the bedroom, and what had it got him? A stab in the chest, a tender liver, and two feet that might as well have been stumps. Paula Turk wasn't born for that sort of life, with its domestic melodrama and greedy sucking babies – no, she was destined for something richer and more complex, something that would define and elevate her, something great. She wanted to compete and she wanted to win – always shining before her like some numinous icon was the glittering image of triumph. And whenever she flagged, whenever a sniffle or the flu ate at her reserves and she hit the wall in the numbing waters of the Pacific or the devilish winds at the top of San Marcos Pass, she pushed herself through it, drove herself with an internal whip that accepted no excuses and made no allowances for the limitations of the flesh. She was twenty-eight years old and she was going to conquer the world.

On the other hand, Jason Barre, the thirty-three-year-old surf-and-dive-shop proprietor she'd been see-ing pretty steadily over the past nine months, didn't really seem to have the fire of competition in him. Both his parents were doctors (and that, as much as anything, had swayed Paula in his favour when they first met), and they'd set him up in his own business, a business that had continuously lost money since its grand opening three years ago. When the waves were breaking, Jason would be at the beach, and when the surf was flat he'd be stationed behind the counter on his tall swivel stool, selling wax remover to bleached-out adolescents who said things like 'gnarly' and 'killer' in their penetrating, adenoidal tones. Jason liked to surf and he liked to breathe the cigarette haze in sports bars, a permanent sleepy-eyed, widemouthed Californian grin on his face, flip-flops on his feet, and his waist encircled by a pair of faded baggy shorts barely held in place by the gentle sag of his belly and the twin anchors of his hipbones.

That was all right with Paula. She told him he should quit smoking, cut down on his drinking, but she didn't harp on it. In truth, she really didn't care all that much – one world-beater in a relationship was enough. When she was in training, which was all the time now, she couldn't help feeling a kind of moral superiority to anyone who wasn't – and Jason most emphatically wasn't. He was no threat and he didn't want to be – his mind just didn't work that way. He was cute, that was all, and just as she got a little *frisson* of pleasure from the swell of his paunch beneath the oversized T-shirt and his sleepy eyes and his laid-back ways, he admired her for her drive and the lean, hard triumph of her beauty and her strength. She never took drugs or alcohol – or hardly ever – but he persuaded her to try just a puff or two of marijuana before they made love, and it seemed to relax her, open up her pores till she could feel her nerve ends poking through them, and their lovemaking was like nothing she'd ever experienced, except maybe breaking the tape at the end of the twenty-six miles of the marathon.

It was a Friday night in August, half-past seven, the sun hanging in the window like a *piñata*, and she'd just stepped out of the shower after a six-hour tuneup for Sunday's triathlon, when the phone rang. Jason's voice came over the wire, low and soft. 'Hey, babe,' he said, breathing into the phone like a sex maniac. (He always called her 'babe', and she loved it, precisely because she wasn't a babe and never would be – it was their little way of mocking the troglodytes moulded into the barstools beside him.)

'Listen, I was just wondering if you might want to join me down at Clubber's for a while. Yeah, I know, you need your sleep and the big day's the day after tomorrow and Zinny Bauer's probably already asleep, but how about it? Come on. It's my birthday.'

'Your birthday? I thought your birthday was in December?'

There was the ghost of a pause during which she could detect the usual wash of background noise, drunken voices crying out as if from the netherworld, the competing announcers of the six different games unfolding simultaneously on the twelve big-screen TVs, the insistent pulse of the jukebox thumping faintly beneath it all. 'No,' he said, 'my birthday's today, August 26th – it is. I don't know when you got the idea it was in December . . . But come on, babe, don't you have to load up on carbohydrates?'

She did. She admitted it. 'I was going to make pancakes and penne,' she said, 'with a little cheese sauce and maybe a loaf of that brown-and-serve bread . . .'

'I'll take you to the Pasta Bowl, all you can eat – and I swear I'll have you back by eleven.' He lowered his voice. 'And no sex, I know – I wouldn't want to drain you or anything.'

She wasn't soft because she ran forty-five miles a week, biked two hundred and fifty, and slashed through fifteen thousand metres of the crawl in the Baños del Mar pool. She was in the best shape of her life, and Saturday's triathlon was nothing, way less than half the total distance of the big one – the Hawaii Ironman – in October. She wasn't soft because she'd finished second in the women's division last year in Hawaii and forty-fourth over all, beating out one thousand, three hundred and fifty other contestants, twelve hundred of whom, give or take a few, were men. Like Jason. Only fitter. A whole lot fitter.

She swung by Clubber's to pick him up – he wasn't driving, not since his last DUI, anyway – and, though parking was no problem, she had to endure the stench of cigarettes and the faint sour odour of yesterday's vomit while he finished his cocktail and wrapped up his ongoing analysis of the Dodgers' chances with an abstract point about a blister on somebody or other's middle finger. The guy they called Little Drake, white-haired at thirty-six and with a face that reminded Paula of one of those naked drooping dogs, leaned out of his Hawaiian shirt and into the radius of Jason's gesticulating hands as if he'd never heard such wisdom in his life. And Paula? She stood there at the bar in her shorts and Lycra halter top, sucking an Evian through a straw while the sports fans furtively admired her pecs and lats and the hard-hammered musculature of her legs, for all the world a babe. She didn't mind. In fact, it made her feel

luminous and alive, not to mention vastly superior to all
those pale lumps of flesh sprouting out of the corners like
toadstools and the sagging abrasive girlfriends who hung
on their arms and tried to feign interest in whatever sport
happened to be on the tube.

But somebody was talking to her – Little Drake, it was
Little Drake, leaning across Jason and addressing her as if
she were one of them. 'So, Paula,' he was saying. 'Paula?'

She swivelled her head toward him, hungry now,
impatient. She didn't want to hang around the bar and
schmooze about Tommy Lasorda and O.J. and Proposi-
tion 187 and how Phil Aguirre had broken both legs and
his collarbone in the surf at Rincon; she wanted to go to
the Pasta Bowl and carbo-load. 'Yes?' she said, trying to
be civil, for Jason's sake.

'You going to put them to shame on Saturday, or
what?'

Jason was snubbing out his cigarette in the ashtray,
collecting his money from the bar. They were on their
way out the door – in ten minutes she'd be forking up
fettuccine or angel hair with black olives and sun-dried
tomatoes while Jason regaled her with a satiric portrait of
his day and all the crazies who'd passed through his shop.
This little man with the white hair didn't require a
dissertation, and, besides, he couldn't begin to appreciate the difference between what she was doing and the
ritualistic farce of the tobacco-spitting, crotch-grabbing
'athletes' all tricked out in their pretty unblemished
uniforms up on the screen over his head, so she just
smiled, like a babe, and said, 'Yeah.'

Truly, the race was nothing, just a warmup, and it
would have been less than nothing but for the puzzling
fact that Zinny Bauer was competing. Zinny was a
professional, from Hamburg, and she was the one

who'd cranked past Paula like some sort of machine in the final stretch of the Ironman last year. What Paula couldn't fathom was why Zinny was bothering with this small-time event when there were so many other plums out there. On the way out of Clubber's, she mentioned it to Jason. 'Not that I'm worried,' she said, 'just mystified.'

It was a fine, soft, glowing night, the air rich with the smell of the surf, the sun squeezing the last light out of the sky as it sank toward Hawaii. Jason was wearing his faded-to-pink 49ers jersey and a pair of shorts so big they made his legs look like sticks. He gave her one of his hooded looks, then got distracted and tapped at his watch twice before lifting it to his ear and frowning. 'Damn thing stopped,' he said. It wasn't until they were sliding into the car that he came back to the subject of Zinny Bauer. 'It's simple, babe,' he said, shrugging his shoulders and letting his face go slack. 'She's here to psych you out.'

He liked to watch her eat. She wasn't shy about it – not like the other girls he'd dated, the ones on a perpetual diet who made you feel like a two-headed hog every time you sat down to a meal, whether it was a Big Mac or the Mexican Plate at La Fondita. No 'salad with dressing on the side' for Paula, no butterless bread or child's portions. She attacked her food like a lumberjack, and you'd better keep your hands and fingers clear. Tonight she started with potato gnocchi in a white sauce puddled with butter, and she ate half a loaf of crusty Italian bread with it, sopping up the left-over sauce till the plate gleamed. Next it was the fettuccine with Alfredo sauce, and on her third trip to the pasta bar she heaped her plate with mostaccioli marinara and chunks of hot sausage – and more bread, always more bread.

He ordered a beer, lit a cigarette without thinking, and shovelled up some spaghetti carbonara, thick on the fork and sloppy with sauce. The next thing he knew, he was staring up into the hot green gaze of the waitperson, a pencil-necked little fag he could have snapped in two like a breadstick if this weren't California and everything so copacetic and laid-back. It was times like this when he wished he lived in Cleveland, even though he'd never been there, but he knew what was coming and he figured people in Cleveland wouldn't put up with this sort of crap.

'You'll have to put that out,' the little fag said.

'Sure, man,' Jason said, gesturing broadly so that the smoke fanned out around him like the remains of a pissed-over fire. 'Just as soon as I' – puff, puff – 'take another drag and' – puff, puff – 'find me an ashtray somewhere . . . you wouldn't happen' – puff, puff – 'to have an ashtray, would you?'

Of course the little fag had been holding one out in front of him all along, as if it were a portable potty or something, but the cigarette was just a glowing stub now, the tiny fag end of a cigarette – fag end, how about that? – and Jason reached out, crushed the thing in the ashtray and said, 'Hey, thanks, dude – even though it really wasn't a cigarette but just the *fag* end of one.'

And then the waiter was gone and Paula was there, her fourth plate of the evening mounded high with angel hair, three-bean salad, and wedges of fruit in five different colours. 'So what was that all about? Your cigarette?'

Jason ignored her, forking up spaghetti. He took a long swig of his beer and shrugged. 'Yeah, whatever,' he said finally. 'One more fascist doing his job.'

'Don't be like that,' she said, using the heel of her bread to chase the beans around the plate.

'Like what?'

'You know what I mean. I don't have to lecture you.'

'Yeah?' He let his eyes droop. 'So what do you call this, then?'

She sighed and looked away, and that sigh really irritated him, rankled him, made him feel like flipping the table over and sailing a few plates through the window. He was drunk. Or three-quarters drunk, anyway. Then her lips were moving again. 'Everybody in the world doesn't necessarily enjoy breathing through a tube of incinerated tobacco, you know,' she said. 'People are into health.'

'Who? You maybe. But the rest of them just want to be a pain in the ass. They just want to abrogate my rights in a public place' – abrogate, now where did that come from? – 'and then rub my nose in it.' The thought soured him even more, and when he caught the waitperson pussyfooting by out of the corner of his eye he snapped his fingers with as much pure malice as he could manage. 'Hey, dude, another beer here, huh? I mean, when you get a chance.'

It was then that Zinny Bauer made her appearance. She stalked through the door like something crossbred in an experimental laboratory, so rangy and hollow-eyed and fleshless she looked as if she'd been pasted on to her bones. There was a guy with her – her trainer or husband or whatever – and he was right out of an X-Men cartoon, all head and shoulders and great big beefy biceps. Jason recognised them from Houston – he'd flown down to watch Paula compete in the Houston race only to see her hit the wall in the run and finish sixth in the women's while Zinny Bauer, the Amazing Bone Woman, took an easy first. And here they were, Zinny and Klaus – or Olaf, or whoever – here in the Pasta

Bowl, carbo-loading like anybody else. His beer came, cold and dependable, green in the bottle, pale amber in the glass, and he downed it in two gulps. 'Hey, Paula,' he said, and he couldn't keep the quick sharp stab of joy out of his voice – he was happy suddenly and he didn't know why. 'Hey, Paula, you see who's here?'

The thing that upset her was that he'd lied to her, the way her father used to lie to her mother, the same way – casually, almost as a reflex. It wasn't his birthday at all. He'd just said that to get her out because he was drunk and he didn't care if she had to compete the day after tomorrow and needed her rest and peace and quiet and absolutely no stimulation whatever. He was selfish, that was all, selfish and unthinking. And then there was the business with the cigarette – he knew as well as anybody in the state that there was an ordinance against smoking in public places as of January last, and still he had to push the limits like some cocky immature chip-on-the-shoulder surfer. Which is exactly what he was. But all that was forgivable – it was the Zinny Bauer business she just couldn't forgive.

Paula wasn't even supposed to be there. She was supposed to be at home, making up a batch of pancakes and penne with cheese sauce and lying inert on the couch with the remote control. This was the night before the night before the event, a time to fuel up her tanks and veg out. But because of him, because of her silver-tongued hero in the baggy shorts, she was at the Pasta Bowl, carbo-loading in public. And so was Zinny Bauer, the last person on earth she wanted to see.

That was bad enough, but Jason made it worse, far worse – Jason made it into one of the most excruciating moments of her life. What happened was purely crazy and if she didn't know Jason better she would have thought he'd planned it. They were squabbling over his cigarette and how unlaid-back and uptight the whole thing had made him – he was drunk, and she didn't appreciate him when he was drunk, not at all – when his face suddenly took on a conspiratorial look and he said, 'Hey, Paula, you see who's here?'

'Who?' she said, and she shot a glance over her shoulder and froze: it was Zinny Bauer and her husband, Armin. 'Oh, shit,' she said, and she lowered her head and focused on her plate as if it were the most fascinating thing she'd ever seen. 'She didn't see me, did she? We've got to go. Right now. Right this minute.'

Jason was smirking. He looked happy about it, as if he and Zinny Bauer were old friends. 'But you've only had four plates, babe,' he said. 'You sure we got our money's worth? I could go for maybe just a touch more pasta – and I haven't even had any salad yet.'

'No joking around, this isn't funny.' Her voice withered in her throat. 'I don't want to see her. I don't want to talk to her. I just want to get out of here, OK?'

His smile got wider. 'Sure, babe, I know how you feel – but you're going to beat her, you are, no sweat. You don't have to let anybody chase you out of your favourite restaurant in your own town – I mean, that's not right, is it? That's not in the spirit of friendly competition.'

'Jason,' she said, and she reached across the table and took hold of his wrist. 'I mean it. Let's get out of here. Now.'

Her throat was constricted, everything she'd eaten about to come up. Her legs ached, and her ankle – the one she'd sprained last spring – felt as if someone had driven a nail through it. All she could think of was Zinny

Bauer, with her long muscles and the shaved blonde stubble of her head and her eyes that never quit. Zinny Bauer was behind her, at her back, right there, and it was too much to bear. '*Jason*,' she hissed.

'OK, OK,' he was saying, and he tipped back the dregs of his beer and reached into his pocket and scattered a couple of rumpled bills across the table to cover the checks. Then he rose from the chair with a slow drunken grandeur and gave her a wink as if to indicate that the coast was clear. She got up, hunching her shoulders as if she could compress herself into invisibility, and stared down at her feet as Jason took her arm and led her across the room – if Zinny saw her, Paula wouldn't know about it, because she wasn't going to look up and she wasn't going to make eye contact, she wasn't.

Or so she thought.

She was concentrating on her feet, on the black-and-white-checked pattern of the floor tiles and how her running shoes negotiated them as if they were attached to somebody else's legs, when all of a sudden Jason stopped and her eyes flew up and she saw that they were hovering over Zinny Bauer's table like casual acquaintances, like neighbours on their way to a PTA meeting. 'But aren't you Zinny Bauer?' Jason said, his voice gone high and nasal as he shifted into his Valley Girl imitation. 'The great triathlete? Oh God, yes, yes, you are, aren't you? Oh, God, could I have your autograph for my little girl?'

Paula was made of stone. She couldn't move, couldn't speak, couldn't even blink her eyes. And Zinny – she looked as if her plane had just crashed. Jason was playing out the charade, pretending to fumble through his pockets for a pen, when Armin broke the silence.

'Why don't you just fock off,' he said, and the veins stood out in his neck.

'Oh, she'll be so thrilled,' Jason went on, his voice pinched to a squeal. 'She's so adorable, only six years old, and, oh my God, she's not going to believe this!'

Armin rose to his feet. Zinny clutched at the edge of the table with bloodless fingers, her eyes narrow and hard. The waiter – the one Jason had been riding – started toward them, crying out, 'Is everything all right?' as if the phrase had any meaning.

And then Jason's voice changed, just like that. 'Fuck you, too, Jack, and your scrawny fucking bald-headed squeeze.'

Armin worked out, you could see that, and Paula doubted he'd ever pressed a cigarette to his lips, let alone a joint, but still Jason managed to hold his own – at least until the kitchen staff separated them. There was some breakage, a couple of chairs overturned, a whole lot of noise and cursing and threatening, most of it from Jason. Every face in the restaurant was drained of colour by the time the kitchen staff came to the rescue, and somebody went to the phone and called the police, but Jason blustered his way out the door and disappeared before they arrived. And Paula? She just melted away and kept on melting until she found herself behind the wheel of the car, cruising slowly down the darkened streets, looking for Jason.

She never did find him.

When he called the next morning, he was all sweetness and apology. He whispered, moaned, sang to her, his voice a continuous soothing current insinuating itself through the line and into her head and right on down through her veins and arteries to the unresisting core of her. 'Listen, Paula, I didn't mean for things to get out of hand,' he whispered, 'you've got to believe me. I just didn't think you had to hide from anybody, that's all.'

She listened, her mind gone numb, and let his words saturate her. It was the day before the event, and she wasn't going to let anything distract her. But then, as he went on, pouring himself into the phone with his penitential, self-pitying tones as if he were the one who'd been embarrassed and humiliated, she felt the outrage coming up in her: didn't he understand, didn't he know what it meant to stare into the face of your own defeat? And over a plate of pasta, no less? She cut him off in the middle of a long digression about some surfing legend of the fifties and all the adversity he'd had to face from a host of competitors, a blood-sucking wife, and a fearsome backwash off Newport Beach.

'What did you think?' she demanded. 'That you were protecting me or something? Is that it? Because if that's what you think, let me tell you I don't need you or anybody else to stand up for me – '

'Paula,' he said, his voice creeping out at her over the wire, 'Paula – I'm on your side, remember? I love what you're doing. I want to help you.' He paused. 'And yes, I want to protect you, too.'

'I don't need it.'

'Yes, you do. You don't think you do, but you do. Don't you see: I was trying to psych her.'

'Psych her? At the Pasta Bowl?'

His voice was soft, so soft she could barely hear him: 'Yeah.' And then, even softer: 'I did it for you.'

It was Saturday, seventy-eight degrees, sun beaming down unmolested, the tourists out in force. The shop had been buzzing since ten, nothing major – cords, tube socks, T-shirts, a couple of illustrated guides to South Coast hot spots that nobody who knew anything needed a book to find – but Jason had been at the cash register right through lunch and on into the four-thirty breathing spell, when the tourist mind tended to fixate on ice-cream cones and those pathetic sidecar bikes they pedalled up and down the street like the true guppies they were. He'd even called Little Drake in to help out for a couple of hours there. Drake didn't mind. He'd grown up rich in Montecito and gone white-haired at twenty-seven, and now he lived with his even whiter-haired old parents and managed their two rental proper-ties downtown – which meant he had nothing much to do except prop up the bar at Clubber's or haunt the shop like the thinnest ghost of a customer. So why not put him to work?

'Nothing to shout about,' Jason told him, over the faint hum of the oldies channel. He leaned back against the wall on his high stool and cracked the first beer of the day. 'Little stuff, but a lot of it. I almost had that one dude sold on the Al Merrick board – I could taste it – but something scared him off. Maybe Mommy took away his Visa card, I don't know.'

Drake pulled contemplatively at his beer and looked out the window at the parade of tourists marching up and down State Street. He didn't respond. It was approaching that crucial hour of the day, the hour known as cocktail hour, two for one, the light struck on the underside of the palms, everything soft and pretty and winding down toward dinner and evening, the whole night held out before them like a promise. 'What time's the Dodger game?' Drake said finally.

Jason looked at his watch. It was a reflex. The Dodgers were playing the Pods at five-thirty, Nomo against

Benes, and he knew the time and channel as well as he knew his ATM number. The Angels were on Prime Ticket, seven-thirty, at home against the Orioles. And Paula – Paula was at home, too, focusing (do not disturb, thank you very much) for the big one with the Amazing Bone Woman the next morning. 'Five-thirty,' he said, after a long pause.

Drake said nothing. His beer was gone, and he shuffled behind the counter to the little reefer for another. When he'd cracked it, sipped, belched, scratched himself thoroughly, and commented on the physique of an overweight Mexican chick in a red bikini making her way up from the beach, he ventured a query on the topic under consideration: 'Time to close up?'

All things being equal, Jason would have stayed open till six, or near six anyway, on a Saturday in August. The summer months accounted for the lion's share of his business – it was like the Christmas season for everybody else – and he tried to maximise it, he really did, but he knew what Drake was saying. Twenty to five now, and they still had to count the receipts, lock up, stop by the night deposit at the B. of A., and then settle in at Clubber's for the game. It would be nice to be there, maybe with a tall tequila tonic and the sports section spread out on the bar, before the game got under way. Just to settle in and enjoy the fruits of their labour. He gave a sigh, for form's sake, and said, 'Yeah, why not?'

And then there was cocktail hour, and he had a couple of tall tequila tonics before switching to beer, and the Dodgers looked good, real good, red hot, and somebody bought him a shot. Drake was carrying on about something – his girlfriend's cat, the calluses on his mother's feet – and Jason tuned him out, ordered two soft chicken tacos and watched the sun do all sorts of amazing pink-and-salmon things to the storefronts across the street before the grey finally settled in. He was thinking he should have gone surfing today, thinking he'd maybe go out in the morning, and then he was thinking of Paula. He should wish her luck or something, give her a phone call, at least. But the more he thought about it, the more he pictured her alone in her apartment power-drinking her fluids, sunk into the shell of her focus like some Chinese Zen master, and the more he wanted to see her.

They hadn't had sex in a week. She was always like that when it was coming down to the wire, and he didn't blame her. Or yes – yes, he did blame her. And he resented it, too. What was the big deal? It wasn't like she was playing ball or anything that took any skill – and why lock him out for that? She was like his overachieving, straight-arrow parents, Type A personalities, early risers, joggers, let's go out and beat the world. God, that was anal. But she had some body on her, as firm and flawless as the Illustrated Man's – or Woman's, actually. He thought about that and about the way her face softened when they were in bed together, and he stood at the pay phone seeing her in the hazy soft-focus glow of some made-for-TV movie. Maybe he shouldn't call. Maybe he should just . . . surprise her.

She answered the door in an oversized sweatshirt and shorts, barefooted, and with the half-full pitcher from the blender in her hand. She looked surprised, all right, but not pleasantly surprised. In fact, she scowled at him and set the pitcher down on the bookcase before pulling back the door and ushering him in. He didn't even get the chance to tell her he loved her or to wish her luck before she started in on him. 'What are you doing here?' she demanded. 'You know I can't see you tonight, of all nights. What's with you? Are you drunk? Is that it?'

What could he say? He stared at the brown gloop in the pitcher for half a beat and then gave her his best simmering droopy-eyed smile and a shrug that radiated down from his shoulders to his hips. 'I just wanted to see you. To wish you luck, you know?' He stepped forward to kiss her, but she dodged away from him, snatching up the pitcher full of gloop like a shield. 'A kiss for luck?' he said.

She hesitated. He could see something go in and out of her eyes, the flicker of a worry, competitive anxiety, butterflies, and then she smiled and pecked him a kiss on the lips that tasted of soy and honey and whatever else was in that concoction she drank. 'Luck,' she said, 'but no excitement.'

'And no sex,' he said, trying to make a joke of it. 'I know.'

She laughed then, a high, girlish tinkle of a laugh that broke the spell. 'No sex,' she said. 'But I was just going to watch a movie, if you want to join me – '

He found one of the beers he'd left in the refrigerator for just such an emergency as this and settled in beside her on the couch to watch the movie – some inspirational crap about a demi-cripple who wins the hurdle event in the Swedish Special Olympics – but he was hot, he couldn't help it, and his fingers kept wandering from her shoulder to her breast, from her waist to her inner thigh. At least she kissed him when she pushed him away. 'Tomorrow,' she promised, but it was only a promise, and they both knew it. She'd been so devastated after the Houston thing she wouldn't sleep with him for a week and a half, strung tight as a bow every time he touched her. The memory of it chewed at him, and he sipped his beer moodily. 'Bullshit,' he said.

'Bullshit what?'

'Bullshit you'll sleep with me tomorrow. Remember Houston? Remember Zinny Bauer?'

Her face changed suddenly and she flicked the remote angrily at the screen and the picture went blank. 'I think you'd better go,' she said.

But he didn't want to go. She was his girlfriend, wasn't she? And what good did it do him if she kicked him out every time some chickenshit race came up? Didn't he matter to her, didn't he matter at all? 'I don't want to go,' he said.

She stood, put her hands on her hips, and glared at him. 'I have to go to bed now.'

He didn't budge. Didn't move a muscle. 'That's what I mean,' he said, and his face was ugly, he couldn't help it. 'I want to go to bed, too.'

Later, he felt bad about the whole thing. Worse than bad. He didn't know how it happened exactly, but there was some resentment there, he guessed, and it just snuck up on him – plus he was drunk, if that was any excuse. Which it wasn't. Anyway, he hadn't meant to get physical, and by the time she'd stopped fighting him and he got her shorts down he hadn't even really wanted to go through with it. This wasn't making love, this wasn't what he wanted. She just lay there beneath him like she was dead, like some sort of zombie, and it made him sick, so sick he couldn't even begin to apologise or excuse himself. He felt her eyes on him as he was zipping up, hard eyes, accusatory eyes, eyes like claws, and he had to stagger into the bathroom and cover himself with the noise of both taps and the toilet to keep from breaking down. He'd gone too far. He knew it. He was ashamed of himself, deeply ashamed, and there really wasn't anything left to say. He just slumped his shoulders and slouched out the door.

And now here he was, contrite and hung over, mooning around on East Beach in the cool hush of 7 a.m., waiting with all the rest of the guppies for the race to start. Paula wouldn't even look at him. Her mouth was set, clamped shut, a tiny little line of nothing beneath her nose, and her eyes looked no further than her equipment – her spidery ultra-lightweight bike with the triathlon bars and her little skullcap of a helmet and water bottles and whatnot. She was wearing a two-piece swimsuit, and she'd already had her number – 23 – painted on her upper arms and the long burnished muscles of her thighs. He shook out a cigarette and stared off past her, wondering what they used for the numbers – Magic Marker? Greasepaint? Something that wouldn't come off in the surf, anyway – or with all the sweat. He remembered the way she'd looked in Houston, pounding through the muggy haze in a sheen of sweat, her face sunk in a mask of suffering, her legs and buttocks taut, her breasts flattened to her chest in the grip of the clinging top. He thought about that, watching her from behind the police line as she bent to fool with her bike, not an ounce of fat on her, nothing, not even a stray hair, and he got hard just looking at her.

But that was short-lived, because he felt bad about last night and knew he'd really have to put himself through the wringer to make it up to her. Plus, just watching the rest of the four hundred and six fleshless masochists parade by with their Gore-Tex T-shirts and Lycra shorts and all the rest of their paraphernalia was enough to make him go cold all over. His stomach felt like a fried egg left out on the counter too long, and his hands shook when he lit the cigarette. He should be in bed, that's where he

should be – enough of this 7 a.m. They were crazy, these
people, purely crazy, getting up at dawn to put themselves through something like this – one mile in the
water, thirty-four on the bike, and a ten-mile run to
wrap it up, and this was a walk compared to the
Ironman. They were all bone and long lean muscle,
like whippet dogs or something, the women indistin-
guishable from the men, stringy and titless. Except for
Paula. She was all right in that department, and that was
genetic – she referred to her breasts as her fat reserves. He
was wondering if they shrank at all during the race, what
with all that stress and water loss, when a woman with
big hair and too much make-up asked him for a light.

She was milling around with maybe a couple of
hundred other spectators – or sadists, he guessed you'd
have to call them – waiting to watch the crazies do their
thing. 'Thanks,' she breathed, after he'd leaned in close
to touch the tip of his smoke to hers. Her eyes were big
wet pools, and she was no freak, no bone woman. Her
lips were wet, too, or maybe it was his imagination. 'So,'
she said, the voice caught low in her throat, a real
smoker's rasp, 'here for the big event?'

He just nodded.

There was a pause. They sucked at their cigarettes. A
pair of gulls flailed sharply at the air behind them and
then settled down to poke through the sand for anything
that looked edible. 'My name's Sandra,' she offered, but
he wasn't listening, not really, because it was then that it
came to him, his inspiration, his moment of grace and
redemption: suddenly, he knew how he was going to
make it up to Paula. He cut his eyes away from the
woman and through the crowd to where Paula bent over
her equipment, the take-no-prisoners look ironed into
her face. And what does she want more than anything?

he asked himself, his excitement so intense he almost
spoke the words aloud. What would make her happy,
glad to see him, ready to party, celebrate, dance till dawn,
and let bygones be bygones?

   To win. That was all. To beat Zinny Bauer. And in
that moment, even as Paula caught his eye and glowered
at him, he had a vision of Zinny Bauer, the Amazing
Bone Woman, coming into the final stretch with her legs
and arms pumping, in command, no problem, and the
bright-green cup of Gatorade held out for her by the
smiling volunteer in the official volunteer's cap and T-
shirt – yes – and Zinny Bauer refreshing herself, drinking
it down in mid-stride, running on and on until she hit
the wall he was already constructing.

Paula pulled the red bathing cap down over her ears,
adjusted her swim goggles, and strode across the beach,
her heartbeat as slow and steady as a lizard's on a cold
rock. She was focused, as clear-headed and certain as
she'd ever been in her life. Nothing mattered now
except leaving all the hotshots and loudmouths and
macho types behind in the dust – and Zinny Bauer,
too. There were a couple of pros competing in the men's
division and she had no illusions about beating them, but
she was going to teach the rest of them a hard lesson, a
lesson about toughness and endurance and will. If
anything, what had happened with Jason last night was
something she could use, the kind of thing that made her
angry, that made her wonder what she'd seen in him in
the first place. He didn't care about her. He didn't care
about anybody. That was what she was thinking when
the gun went off and she hit the water with the great
thundering herd of them, the image of his bleary
apologetic face burning into her brain – date rape, that's

what they called it — and she came out of the surf just behind Zinny Bauer, Jill Eisen, and Tommy Roe, one of the men's pros.

All right, OK. She was on her bike now, through the gate in a flash and driving down the flat wide concourse of Cabrillo Boulevard in perfect rhythm, effortless, as if the blood were flowing through her legs and into the bike itself. Before she'd gone half a mile, she knew she was going to catch Zinny Bauer and pass her to ride with the men's leaders and get off first on the run. It was preordained, she could feel it, feel it pounding in her temples and in the perfect engine of her heart. The anger had settled in her legs now, a bitter, hot-burning fuel. She fed on the air, tucked herself into the handlebars, and flew. If all this time she'd raced for herself, for something uncontainable inside her, now she was racing for Jason, to show him up, to show him what she was, what she really was. There was no excuse for him. None. And she was going to win this event, she was going to beat Zinny Bauer and all those hundreds of soft, winded, under-trained, crowing, chest-thumping jocks, too, and she was going to accept her trophy and stride right by him as if he didn't exist, because she wasn't soft, she wasn't, and he was going to find that out once and for all.

By the time he got back to the beach, Jason thought he'd run some sort of race himself. He was breathing hard — got to quit smoking — and his tequila headache was heating up to the point where he was seriously con-sidering ducking into Clubber's and slamming a shot or two, though it was only half-past nine and all the tourists would be there, buttering their French toast and would you pass the syrup, please, and thank you very much. He'd had to go all the way out to Drake's place and shake

him awake to get the Tuinol – one of Drake's mother's
six thousand and one prescriptions to fight off the
withering aches of her seventy-odd years. Tuinol,
Nembutal, Dalmane, Darvocet: Jason didn't care, just
so long as there was enough of it. He didn't do
barbiturates any more – probably hadn't swallowed a
Tooey in ten years – but he remembered the sweet
numb glow they gave him and the way they made his
legs feel like treetrunks planted deep in the ground.

The sun had burned off the fog by now, and the day was
clear and glittering on the water. They'd started the race at
seven-thirty, so that gave him a while yet – the first men
would be crossing the finish line in just under three hours,
and the women would be coming in at three-ten, three-
twelve, something like that. All he needed to do now was
finesse himself into the inner sanctum, pick up a stray T-
shirt and cap, find the Gatorade, and plant himself about
two miles from the finish. Of course, there was a chance
the Amazing Bone Woman wouldn't take the cup from
him, especially if she recognised him from the other night,
but he was going to pull his cap down low and hide behind
his Ray-Bans and show her a face of devotion. One
second, that's all it would take. A hand coming out of
the crowd, the cup beaded with moisture and moving
right along beside her so she didn't even have to break
stride – and what was there to think about? She drinks and
hits the wall. And if she didn't go for it the first time, he'd
hop in the car and catch her a mile farther on.

He'd been watching one of the security volunteers
stationed outside the trailer that served as a command
centre. A kid of eighteen, maybe, greasy hair, an oversized cross dangling from one ear, a scurf of residual acne.
He was a carbon copy of the kids he sold wetsuits and
Killer Beeswax to – maybe he was even one of them.

Jason reminded himself to tread carefully. He was a businessman, after all, one of the pillars of the downtown community, and somebody might recognise him. But then so what if they did? He was volunteering his time, that was all, a committed citizen doing his civic best to promote tourism and everything else that was right in the world. He ducked under the rope. 'Hey, bro,' he said to the kid, extending his hand for the high five – which the kid gave him. 'Sorry I'm late. Jeff around?'

The kid's face opened up in a big beaming half-witted grin. 'Yeah, sure – I think he went up the beach a ways with Everardo and Linda and some of the press people, but I could maybe look if you want – '

Jeff. It was a safe bet – no crowd of that size, especially one consisting of whippets, bone people, and guppies, would be without a Jeff. Jason gave the kid a shrug. 'Nah, that's all right. But hey, where's the T-shirts and caps at?'

Then he was in his car, and forget the DUI, the big green waxed cup cold between his legs, breaking Tuinol caps and looking for a parking space along the course. He pulled in under a huge Monterey pine that was like its own little city and finished doctoring the Gatorade, stirring the stuff in with his index finger. What would it take to make the Bone Woman's legs go numb and wind up a Did Not Finish without arousing suspicion? Two? Three? He didn't want her to pass out on the spot or take a dive into the bushes or anything, and he didn't want to hurt her, either, not really. But four – four was a nice round number, and that ought to do it. He sucked the finger he'd used as a swizzle stick to see if he could detect the taste, but he couldn't. He took a tentative sip. Nothing. Gatorade tasted like such shit anyway, who could tell the difference?

He found a knot of volunteers in their canary-yellow T-shirts and caps and stationed himself a hundred yards up the street from them, the ice rattling as he swirled his little green time bomb around the lip of the cup. The breeze was soft, the sun caught in the crowns of the trees and reaching out to finger the road here and there in long slim swatches. He'd never tell Paula, of course, no way, but he'd get giddy with her, pop the champagne cork, and let her fill him with all the ecstasy of victory.

A cheer from the crowd brought him out of his reverie. The first of the men was cranking his way around the long bend in the road, a guy with a beard and wraparound sunglasses – the Finn. He was the one favoured to win, or was it the Brit? Jason tucked the cup behind his back and faded into the crowd, which was pretty sparse here, and watched the guy propel himself past, his mouth gaping black, the two holes of his nostrils punched deep into his face, his head bobbing on his neck as if it weren't attached right. Another guy appeared around the corner just as the Finn passed by, and then two others came slogging along behind him. Somebody cheered, but it was a pretty feeble affair.

Jason checked his watch. It would be five minutes or so, and then he could start watching for the Amazing Bone Woman, tireless freak that she was. And did she fuck Klaus, or Olaf, or whoever he was, the night before the big event, or was she like Paula, all focus and negativity and no, no, no? He fingered the cup lightly, reminding himself not to damage or crease it in any way – it had to look pristine, fresh-dipped from the bucket – and he watched the corner at the end of the street till his eyes began to blur from the sheer concentration of it all.

Two more men passed by and nobody cheered, not a murmur, but then suddenly a couple of middle-aged

women across the street set up a howl, and the crowd
chimed in: the first woman, a woman of string and bone
with a puffing heaving puppetlike frame, was swinging
into the street in distant silhouette. Jason moved forward.
He tugged reflexively at the bill of his hat, jammed the
rims of the shades back into his eyesockets. And he
started to grin, all his teeth on fire, his lips spread wide:
Here, take me, drink me, have me!

As the woman drew closer, loping, sweating, elbows
flailing and knees pounding, the crowd getting into it
now, cheering her, cheering this first of the women in a
man's event, the first Ironwoman of the day, he began to
realise that this wasn't Zinny Bauer at all. Her hair was
too long, and her legs and chest were too full – and then
he saw the number clearly, No. 23, and looked into
Paula's face. She was fifty yards from him, but he could
see the toughness in her eyes and the tight little frozen
smile of triumph and superiority. She was winning. She
was beating Zinny Bauer and Jill Eisen and all those
pathetic jocks labouring up the hills and down the
blacktop streets behind her. This was her moment, this
was it.

But then, and he didn't stop to think about it, he
stepped forward, right out on the street where she could
see him, and held out the cup. He heard her feet beating
at the pavement with a hard merciless slap, saw the icy
twist of a smile and the cold triumphant eyes. And he felt
the briefest fleeting touch of her flesh as the cup left his
hand.

Harald, Claudia, and Their Son Duncan
Nadine Gordimer

Something terrible happened.

They are watching it on the screen with their after-dinner coffee cups beside them. It is Bosnia or Somalia or the earthquake shaking a Japanese island like a dog between apocalyptic teeth; whatever were the disasters of that time. The screen serves them up with coffee every night. When the intercom buzzes each looks to the other with a friendly reluctance: you go, your turn. It's part of the covenant of living together. They made the decision to give up the house and move into this town-house complex with grounds maintained and security-moni-tored entrance only recently and they are not yet accustomed, or rather are inclined momentarily to forget that it's not the barking of Robbie and the old-fangled ring of the front door bell that summons them, now. No pets allowed in the complex, but luckily there was the solution that theirs could go to their son who has a garden cottage.

He/she – twitch of a smile, he got himself up with languor directed at her and went to lift the nearest receiver. Who, she half-heard him say, half-listening to the commentary following the images, Who. It could be someone wanting to convert them to some religious sect, or the delivery of a summons for a parking offence; moonlighting workers did this. He said something else she didn't catch but she heard the release buzzer he pressed.

Do you know who Julian Verster might be? Friend of Duncan?

He/she – they didn't, either of them. Nothing unusual about that. Duncan, thirty years old, had his own circle just as his parents had theirs, and these intersected only occasionally where interests, inculcated in him as a child by his parents, met.

What does he want?

Just said to speak to us.

Both at the same instant were touched by a live voltage of alarm. What is there to fear, defined in the known context of a thirty year old in this city – a car crash, a street mugging, a violent break-in at the cottage. Both stood at the door, confronting these, confronting the footsteps they followed approaching up their private paved pathway beneath the crossed swords of Strelitzia palm leaves, the signal of the second buzzer, and this young man come from? For? Duncan. It doesn't matter what he looked like. He stared at the floor as he came in, so they couldn't read him. He sat down without a word; it was an injunction for them to do so, too.

He/she – whose turn. There's been an accident? – she's a doctor, she sees what the ambulances bring into Intensive Care. If something's broken she can gauge whether it ever can be put together again.

This Julian draws the flaps of his lips in over his teeth and clamps his mouth before he speaks.

A kind of . . . Not Duncan, no no! Someone's been shot. Duncan, he's been arrested.

They stand up. For God's sake – what are you talking about – What is all this – How arrested, arrested for what –

The messenger is attacked, he becomes sullen, unable to bear what he has to tell. The obscene word comes ashamedly from him.

Murder.

Everything has come to a stop.

What can be understood is only a car crash, a street mugging, a violent break-in.

He/she. He strides over and switches off the television. And expels a violent breath. So long as nobody moved, nobody uttered, the word and the act within the word could not enter here. Now with the touch of a switch and the gush of breath a new calendar is opened. The old Gregorian cannot register this day. It does not exist in that means of measure.

This Julian now tells them that a magistrate was called 'after hours' (he gives the detail with the weight of its urgent gravity) to lay a charge at the police station and bail was refused. That is the practical purpose of this visit: Duncan says – Duncan says, Duncan's message is that there's no point in their coming, there's no point in trying for bail, he will appear in court on Monday morning. He has his own lawyer.

He/she. She has marked the date on patients' prescriptions dozens of times since morning but she turns to find a question that will bring some kind of answer to that word pronounced by the messenger. She cries out. *What day is it today?*

Friday.

It was on a Friday.

It is probable that neither of the Linmeyers had ever been in a court before. During the forty-eight hours of the weekend of waiting they had gone over every explanation possible in the absence of being able to talk to him, their son, himself. Because of the preposterousness of the charge they felt they had to respect his instruction that they not try to see him; this must indicate that the whole business was ridiculous, that's it, horribly ridiculous, his own ridiculous affair soon to be resolved, better not given the confirmation of being taken seriously by mother and father arriving at a prison accompanied by their lawyer, high emotions, etc. That was the way they brought themselves to read his injunction; a mixture between consideration of them – no need to be mixed up in the business – and the independence of the young he had been granted in mutual understanding and asserted since he was an adolescent.

But dread attends the unknown. Dread was a drug that came to them both not out of something administered from her pharmacopoeia; they calmly walked without anything to say to one another along the corridors of the courts, Harald standing back for his wife Claudia with the politeness of a stranger as they found the right court door, entered and shuffled clumsily sideways to be seated on the fixed benches.

The very smell of the place was that of a foreign country to which they were deported: the odour of polished wooden barriers and highly waxed floor. The windows high above, sloping down their searchlights. The uniforms occupied by men with the impersonality of cult members, all interchangeable wearers of the garb. The presence of a few figures seated somewhere near, the kind who stare from park benches or lie face-down in public gardens. The mind flutters from what confronts it, as a bird that has flown into a confined space does from wall to wall, there must be an opening. Harald collided against awareness of school, too far back to be consciously remembered; institutional smell and hard wood under his buttocks. Even the name of a master was blundered into; nothing from the past could be more remote than this present. In a flick of attention he saw

Claudia rouse from her immobility to disconnect the
beeper that kept her in touch with her surgery. She felt
the distraction and turned her head to read his oblique
glance: nothing. She gave the stiff smile with which one
greets somebody one isn't sure one knows.

He comes up from the well of a stairway between two
policemen. Duncan. Can it be? He has to be recognised
in a persona that doesn't belong to him as they knew
him, have always known him – and who could identify
him better? He is wearing dark-green jeans and a black
cotton sweater. The kind of clothes he customarily
wears, but the neat collar of a white shirt is turned
down outside the neck of the sweater; this is the detail,
token submission to the conventions expected by a
court, that makes the connection of reality between
the one they knew, *him*, and this other, flanked by
policemen.

A blast of heat came over Harald, confusion like
anxiety or anger, but neither. Some reaction that never
before had had occasion to be called up.

Duncan, yes. He looked at them, acknowledging
himself. Claudia smiled at him with lifted head, for
everyone to see. And he inclined his head to her. But
he did not look at his parents directly again during the
proceedings that followed, except as his controlled,
almost musing glance swept over them as it went round
the public gallery across the two young black men with
their legs sprawled relaxedly before them, the old white
man sitting forward with his head in his hands, and the
family group, probably wandered in bewilderedly to pass
the time before a case that concerned them came up, who
were whispering among themselves of their own affairs.

The judge made his stage entrance, everyone fidgeted
to their feet, sank again. The judge was tall or short, bald

or not – doesn't matter; there was the hitch of shoulders under the voluminous gown and, his hunch lowered over papers presented to him, he made a few brief comments in the tone of questions addressed to the tables in the well of the court where the backs of the prosecutor and defence lawyer presented themselves to the gallery. Under ladders of light tilting down, policemen on errands came in and out, conferring in hoarse whispers; the rote of proceedings was concluded. The case was remanded to a date two weeks later. A second application for bail was refused.

Over. But beginning. The parents approached the barrier between the gallery and the court enclosure and were not prevented from contact with their son. Each embraced him while he kept his head turned away from their faces.

Do you need anything?

It's just not on, the young lawyer was saying. I'm serving notice to contest the refusal, right away, right now, Duncan. I won't let the prosecutor get away with it. Don't worry. – This last said to her, the doctor, in exactly the tone of reassurance she herself would use with patients of whose prognosis she herself was uncertain.

The son had an air of impatience, the shifting gaze of one who wished the well-meaning to leave; an urgent need of some preoccupation, business with himself. They could take it to mean confidence; of his innocence – of course; or it could be a cover for dread, akin to the dread they had felt, concealing his dread out of pride, not wanting to be associated with theirs. He was now officially an accused, on record as such. The accused has a status of dread that is his own, hasn't he!

Nothing?

I'll see to everything Duncan needs – the lawyer squeezed his client's arm as he swung a briefcase and was off.

If there was nothing, then . . .

Nothing. Nothing they could ask, not *What is it all about*, what is it that you did; you are supposed to have done?

His father held and expelled a breath again as he had when he switched off the TV set. Is he really a competent enough lawyer? We could get someone else. Anyone.

A good friend and a good lawyer.

Well, I'll be in touch with him later, find out what happened when he saw the prosecutor.

The son will know that his father means money: he'll be ready to supply surety for the contingency that it is impossible to believe has arisen between them, money for bail.

He turns away – the prisoner, that's what he is now – in anticipation of the policemen's move to order him to. He doesn't want them to touch him, he has his own volition, and his mother's clasp just catches the ends of his fingers as he goes.

They see him led down the stairwell to whatever is there beneath the court. As they make to leave Court B17 they become aware that the other friend, the messenger Julian, has been standing just behind them, to assure Duncan of his presence but not wanting to intrude upon those with the closest claims. They greet him and walk out together but do not speak. He feels guilty about his mission, that night, and hurries ahead out of their sight.

As the couple emerge into the foyer of the courts, vast and lofty cathedral echoing with the susurration of its different kind of supplicants gathered there, Claudia suddenly breaks away, disappearing towards the sign indicating toilets. Harald waits for her among these people patient in trouble, no choice to be otherwise, for them; he is one of them, the wives, husbands, fathers, lovers, children of forgers, thieves and murderers. He looks at his watch. The whole process has taken exactly one hour and seven minutes. She returns and they quit the place,

Let's have a coffee somewhere.

Oh . . . There are patients at the surgery, expecting me.

Let them wait.

She did not have time to get to the lavatory and vomited in the washroom basin. There was no warning; trooping out with all those other people in trouble, part of the anxious and stunned gait, she suddenly felt the clenching of her insides and knew what was going to come. She did not tell him, when she rejoined him, and he must have assumed she had gone to the place for the usual purpose. Medically, there was an explanation for such an attack coming on without nausea. Extreme tension could trigger the seizure of muscles. 'Vomited her heart out': that was the expression some of her patients used when describing the symptom. She had always received it, drily, as dramatically inaccurate.

Let them wait.

What he was saying was to hell with them, the patients, how can their pains and aches and pregnancies compare with this? Everything came to a stop, that night; everything has come to a stop. In the coffee bar an androgynous waiter with long curly hair tied back and tennis-ball biceps hummed his pleasure along with piped

music. In the mortuary there was lying the body of a
man. They ordered a filter coffee (Harald) and a
cappuccino (Claudia). The man who was shot in the
head, found dead. Why should it be unexpected that it
was a man? Was not that a kind of admission, already,
credence that it could have been done at all? To assume
that the body would represent a woman, a woman killed
out of jealous passion, the most common form of the act,
one from the sensational pages of the Sunday papers,
crime passionnel, was to accept the possibility that it was
committed, *entered at all* into a life's context. *His*. Road
accidents, plane crashes, the random violence of night
streets, these are the hazards that belong there, the
contemporary version of what people used to believe
in as fate, along with the given eternals, the risks of
illness, failure of ambition, loss of love. These are what
those responsible for an existence recognise they have
exposed it to.

We're not much the wiser.

She didn't answer. Her eyebrows lifted as she reached
for the packets of sugar. Her hand was trembling slightly,
privately, from the recent violent convulsion of her
body. If he noticed he did not remark on it.

They now understood what they had expected from
him: outrage at the preposterous – thing – accusation, laid
upon him. Against his presence there between two
policemen before a judge. They had expected to have
him burst forth at the sight of them; that was what they
were ready for, to tell them – what? Whatever he could,
within the restriction of that room with policemen
hovering and clerks scratching papers together and the
gallery hangers-on dawdling past. That his being there
was crazy, they must get him out immediately, impor-
tune officials, protest – what? Tell them. Tell them.

Some explanation. How it could be thought that this situation was possible.

A good friend.

The lawyer a good friend. And that was all. His back as he went down the stairwell, a policeman on either side. Now, while Harald stretched a leg so that he could reach coins in his trouser pocket, *he* was in a confine they had never seen, a cell. The body of a man was in the mortuary. Harald left a tip for the young waiter who was humming. The petty rituals of living are a daze of continuity over what has come to a stop.

They were walking to their car through the continuum of the city, separated and brought side by side again by the narrowing and widening of the pavements in relation to other people going about their lives, the vendors' spread stocks of small pyramids of vegetables, chewing gum, sunglasses and second-hand clothes, the gas burners on which sausages like curls of human gut were frying.

In the afternoon she couldn't let them wait. It was the day come round for her weekly stint at a clinic. Doctors like herself, in private practice, were expected to meet this need in areas of the city and the once genteel white suburbs of Johannesburg where now there was an influx, a rise in and variety of the population. Now conscientiousness goaded her, over what had come to a stop; she went to her clinic instead of accompanying Harald to the lawyer. Perhaps this also was to keep herself to the conviction that what had happened could not be? It was not a day to examine motives; just follow the sequence set out in an appointment register. She put on her same white coat (she's a functionary, as the judge is, hunched in his robe) and entered the institutional

domain familiar to her, the steaming steriliser with its
battery of precise instruments for every task, the dancing
show of efficiency of the young district nurse with her
doll's starched white crown pinned at the top of her
dreadlocks.

The procession of flesh was laid before the doctor. It
was her medium, in which she worked, the abundant
black thighs reluctantly parted in modesty (the nurse
chaffed the women, *Ma-gogo*, Doctor's a woman just like
you), the white hairy paps of old men under auscultation.
The babies' tender bellies slid under her palms; tears of
terrible reproach bulged from their eyes when she had to
thrust the needle into the soft padding of their upper
arms, where muscle had not yet developed. She did it as
she performed any necessary procedure, with all her skill
to avoid pain.

Isn't that the purpose?

There is plenty of pain that arises from within; this
woman with a tumour growing in her neck, plain to feel
it under experienced fingers, and then the usual weekly
procession of pensioners hobbled by arthritis.

But the pain inflicted from without – the violation of
the flesh, a child is burned by an overturned pot of
boiling water, or a knife is thrust. A bullet. This piercing
of the flesh, the force, ram of a bullet deep into it, steel
alloy that breaks bone as if shattering a teacup – she is not
a surgeon but in this violent city she has watched those
nuggets delved for and prised out on operating tables;
they retain the streamline shape of velocity itself, there is
no element in the human body that can withstand, even
dent, a bullet – those who survive recall the pain
differently from one another but all accounts agree: an
assault. The pain that is the product of the body itself, its
malfunction, is part of the self; somewhere, a mystery

medical science cannot explain, the self is responsible. But this – the bullet in the head: the pure assault of pain.

The purpose of a doctor's life is to defend the body against the violence of pain. She stands on the other side of the divide from those who wilfully cause it. The divide of the ultimate, between death and life.

This body whose interior she is exploring with a plastic-gloved hand like a diviner's instinctively led to a hidden water-source has a foetus, three months of life inside it.

I'm telling you true, Doctor. I was never so sick with the others. Every morning, sick like a dog.

Vomit your heart out.

D'you think that means it's a boy, Doctor? The patient has the mock coyness women often affect towards a doctor; the consulting room is their stage for a little performance. Ag, my husband'd be over the moon for a boy. But I tell him, if we don't do it right this time, I don't know about you, but I'm giving up.

The doctor obliges by laughing with her.

We could do a simple test if you want to know the sex.

Oh no, it's God's will.

Life staggers along powered by worn bellows of old people's lungs and softly pulses between the ribs of a skinny small boy. For some, what is prescribed is denied them by circumstances outside their control. Green vegetables and fresh fruit – they are too poor for the luxury of these remedies; what they have come to the doctor for is a magical bottle of medicine. She knows this but has ready a supply of diet sheets which propose meals made with various pulses as some sort of substitute for what they should be able to eat. She hands a sheet encouragingly to the woman who has brought her two

grandchildren to the doctor. Their scarred grey-filmed
black legs are bare, but despite the heat they watch the
doctor from under thick woollen caps that cover the
sores on their heads and come down right to the
eyebrows. The woman studies the sheet slowly at arm's
length in the manner of ageing people becoming far-
sighted. She folds it carefully. Her time is up. She
shepherds the children to the door. She thanks the
doctor. I don't know if I can get. Maybe I can try buy
some these things. The father, he's still in jail. My son.

Charge sheet. Indictment. Harald kept himself at a
remove of cold attention in order to separate what was
evidence from interpretation of that evidence. Circumstantial evidence: that day, that night, Friday 19th
January, 1996, a man was found dead in a house he
shared with two other men. David Baker and Nkululeko
'Kulu' Dladla came home at 6.45 p.m. and found the
body of their friend Carl Jespers in the living room. He
had a bullet wound in the head. He was lying half-on,
half-off a sofa, as if (Interpretation) he had been taken by
surprise when shot and had tried to rise. He was wearing
thonged sandals, one of which was twisted hanging off
his foot, and above a pair of shorts was naked. There
were two glasses on an African drum that served as a table
beside the sofa. One held the dregs of what appeared to
have been a mixture known as a Bloody Mary – an
empty tin of tomato juice and a bottle of vodka were on
top of the television set. The other glass was apparently
unused; there was an opened bottle of whisky and a
bucket of half-melted ice on a tray on the floor beside the
drum. (Circumstantial combined with Interpretation.)
There was no unusual disorder in the room; this is a
bachelor household. (Interpretation.) The room was in

darkness except for the pinpoint of light from the CD player that had come to the end of a disc and not been disconnected. The front door was locked but glass doors which led to the garden were open. (Circumstantial.)

The garden is one in which a cottage is sited. The house is the main dwelling on a property common to both. The cottage is occupied by Duncan Linmeyer, a mutual friend of the dead man and the two men who discovered him, and they ran to Linmeyer after they had seen Jespers' body. Linmeyer's dog was asleep outside the cottage and it appeared that there was no one at home. When the police came about twenty minutes later they searched the garden and found a gun in a clump of fern. Baker and Dladla identified it as the gun kept in the house as mutual protection against burglars; neither could recall in whose of their three names it was licensed, if at all. A plumber's assistant, Petrus Muchanga, who occupied an outhouse on the property in exchange for part-time work in the garden, was questioned and said that he had seen Linmeyer come out on the verandah of the house and drop something as he crossed the garden to the cottage. Muchanga thought he would retrieve it for him but could not find anything. Linmeyer had already entered his cottage. Muchanga does not own a watch. He could not say what time this was; the sun was down. The police then proceeded to the cottage. There was no response to the bell or knocking on the front door, but Muchanga insisted that Linmeyer was inside. The police effected entry by forcing the kitchen door and found that Linmeyer was in the bedroom. He seemed dazed. He said he had been asleep. Asked whether he knew his friend Carl Jespers had been attacked, he went 'white in the face' (Interpretation) and demanded, Is he dead?

Fingerprint tests were inconclusive because Muchanga had recently watered the clump of fern. The fingerprints on the gun were largely obliterated by mud.

This is not a detective story. Harald has to understand that the mode of events that genre represents is actuality, this is the sequence of circumstantial evidence and interpretation by which a charge of murder is arrived. It is a matter of patricide and matricide. On Friday 19th January, 1996. He/she.

The Drowned Son
David Guterson

Hutchinson's son died in October. He and another man aboard the gill-netter *Fearless* went down in sixty-five-knot winds at a place known as Cape Fox. The other man lived, but Paul had died; he was lost at sea, permanently missing beneath the waves. The news came to Hutchinson and his wife in the form of a phone call, followed by a fax, from the Coast Guard base in Ketchikan, Alaska.

The day the news arrived, Hutchinson had gone duck hunting and had shot his limit by eleven-thirty. While his wife was speaking to the Coast Guard chief petty officer, Hutchinson was on the road between Vantage and Ellensburg, headed westward toward the mountains and Seattle, and feeling keenly the pleasure of his existence – three greenheads and a mallard hen in the cooler behind him, his dog asleep with her head on her paws, a thermos of coffee wedged against the dashboard, the grey reaching sageland outside. While he rolled through Rye Pass and into the Ellensburg Valley his wife read the fax message half a dozen times. Later she mulled over all the picture albums, starting with Paul as a swaddled infant and working her way forward. She found many photos from hunting expeditions, and she realised she couldn't view these without bitterness. She pondered Paul holding his first duck by the neck, smiling numbly at the camera.

While his wife lingered over photo albums, Hutchinson drank coffee and watched a football game at the Sportsman's Café in Cle Elum. There were perhaps a dozen other men present – smoking, drinking, staring silently at the screen – and Hutchinson found that the sullen, hung-over atmosphere of the place dissipated the spirit opening up in him all morning. He took a booth and, with the sports section propped against a napkin dispenser, ate two eggs, hash browns, sausage, and sourdough toast spread with blackberry jam. Now, six weeks later, it was the last decent meal he could remember eating. It had sat nicely in his gut. He'd cleaned up thoroughly with cold canteen water, then driven through Snoqualmie Pass under a cool, pale sky, Tess wide awake and panting by the window, fall sunlight washing the mountainsides. The pass was clear and windy that afternoon, and Hutchinson drove through it certain it was a good thing to arrive home early on a Saturday in October: he would have ample time to get his things put away; he would draw, pluck, and roast two of his ducks.

His wife met him at the door with the news, and Hutchinson, not believing it for a moment, hurried into his house to read the death notice from the Coast Guard.

They were eating dinner. There was no such thing as dinner. Hutchinson and his wife had both stopped cooking. She lived on slices of cheese.

'You can say that,' Hutchinson was saying. 'You can accuse me of that. But I don't think it's really fair.'

He propped himself against the stove. In one hand he held a large spoon aloft and in the other he held a soup pot. His wife was at the table with a box of cornflakes in front of her.

'They say this happens,' he reminded his wife. 'Turns out true, doesn't it.'

'Maybe, maybe not,' she answered. 'But either way, it's an observation I'm not really interested in.'

'Oh,' said Hutchinson.

'Oh,' said his wife. 'Jesus.'

He didn't eat the soup. 'I'm guilty,' he told her. 'Yes, I blame myself. Say what you want. Go ahead. I blame you, too, you know. We blame each other.'

She got up. She didn't look at him. She was very much this sort of woman and he had always known that. 'What you say about me is true,' he confessed. 'But you babied him, Laura. If you hadn't babied him he wouldn't have felt like a coward. Everybody's guilty of something, you know. We both made our contributions.'

'I'm just so sick of listening to you squirm,' answered Laura. 'It isn't worth it any more.'

She left the kitchen. He ate his soup. He stood at the stove with the soup in his mouth and knew himself disposed to feel like a coward, too: it was painful and embarrassing to think on. His own father, Paul's grandfather, had been a coward. Hutchinson understood that his own heart had shaped itself in response to his father's heart. But what boy's doesn't? What man's doesn't? It did not seem to him a bad thing, in general, to be who he was. He still believed in himself. His doubts were normal.

He insisted to himself that it was her fault, in part her fault, for not concurring with him about the need to assist Paul in the evolution of his fortitude. She had long resisted this notion. The boy had been born with a wavering at the core that Hutchinson understood. It needed work, was all. It needed consistent attention, and nothing counterproductive. So she, Laura, was a part of

it. She had to see that. Then they could go forward
together to suffer their punishment and to move,
conjoined, toward redemption.

When he heard her step coming back down the
hallway he stood holding the pot again, not eating. He
leaned against the stove and observed for the thousandth
time that her grieving made her unattractive. He wanted
to be in bed with her, unclothed, smelling the shadow
between her breasts. 'I think I want you to leave,' she
said. 'I can't stand the sight of you any more.'

A week before Christmas he gave her to understand over
the telephone that he was entitled to see his own
daughter who was home from UCLA. His wife told
him the date to come for dinner and he wrote it in capital
letters on his desk calendar and then sketched a red heart
with an arrow through it.

'I love you,' he said. 'I want you to know that.'

'All right,' she answered. 'You love me.'

The man who had worked with Paul aboard the *Fearless*
was standing in the living room with a bourbon and
water when Hutchinson came over for dinner. 'I'm Bob
Pomeroy,' he said, extending his hand. 'I knew your son,
Paul.'

The man didn't look like a fisherman. He was neither
rugged nor large. His wire-rimmed glasses sat cockeyed
on his nose, the line of his chin was too delicate. How
had this man survived? thought Hutchinson. He didn't
have the look of a survivor. His threadbare shirt was
stained with house paint, he blinked often, his lips were
cracked.

They sat at the table in the dining room. Hutchinson's
daughter had gained ten pounds and had changed the

style of her hair: a pageboy. She wore a pastel smock with velvet tights and coolly drank a glass of white wine. Her legs crossed, her glasses on a chain against her flat chest. She was majoring, she said, in computer science and taking classes in finance.

When all the things were on the dining-room table Bob Pomeroy spoke. 'I'm glad I came,' he said.

'We are, too,' answered Hutchinson. 'We tried to get in touch with you. We – '

'I couldn't,' said Bob Pomeroy. 'I couldn't bring myself.'

'You should have, you know,' said Hutchinson. 'What was stopping you?'

Bob Pomeroy shook his head and pressed his glasses against his nose with a dry, cracked forefinger. 'It wasn't possible,' he said. 'I'm sorry.'

Hutchinson leaned toward him across the surface of the table. 'You didn't think we wanted to hear from you?' he said. 'You didn't think we wondered every day? Didn't you try to see things from our point of view? Didn't you realise what was happening?'

'Look,' answered Bob Pomeroy firmly, 'this is ugly, Mr Hutchinson. This is going to be painful. There's a lot I'm going to have to lay on you before I leave here tonight.'

He met Hutchinson's gaze then – watery eyes behind wire-rimmed glasses – and Hutchinson sat back, his heart wavering. 'I'll tell you the whole story,' said the fisherman. 'It's like my duty to Paul to tell you everything.'

The *Fearless*, Bob explained, was primarily a salmon boat, geared to gill net or to troll, depending. Bob's habit was to run the Inside Passage from Seattle to Juneau mid-April, troll from the Pedro Grounds to Cape Chirikoff through mid-June, then work the net through the height of the Alaskan summer, when dusk sits purple on the waters until one in the morning and a fine dawn comes softly at three. Early September was boom time for dog salmon, and in a good year they held until the end of the month; then, depending on how lucky Bob was feeling, or how desperate his need for money was, he either hung around and fished until it was entirely pointless or hung it up and steamed south before the big weather brewed. The middle of October was late for going home.

Some bad things had happened this season. He'd gone through a lot of foul, nasty weather, doubling and even tripling up a lot of three-quarter-inch lines that chafed through inside of a week's time. A good net sunk, the fishing had been poor, and he'd passed a lot of good hours tied to floats. In mid-July his girlfriend of two years took flight. She got off at Port Chilikoot, just south of Haines, and refused to come back on board. They argued outside a house on the old army post with the wind screaming in their faces. Bob was one of life's losers, she said: she had to get on with her life. Then she shut the door to the house, and that was the end of the matter.

The result was that Bob had to find a new deckhand, which he did by steaming up to Skagway. In a tourist saloon he turned up Hutchinson's son, who was nineteen and a half and weighed two hundred pounds: precisely at that juncture in his earthly existence when he would be capable of pushing his body hardest. Bo Pomeroy, who was fifteen years older, knew this exceedingly well. The boy was strong and, more than that, eager – though he exerted himself to couch the adolescent surface of his zeal in an adult's knowingness and ease. He was healthy and well fed. He'd driven north from Seattle in a pickup truck, accompanied by a high-school wrestling buddy who had eventually abandoned him for work on a halibut schooner. He had wanted an adventure on the AlCan Highway, he had wanted to be a reckless knockabout, but of course, Bob knew he was only a kid who would go to college one day, to a state university where a lot of beer got drunk in dormitory rooms and fraternity house hallways. In the meantime, here he was in the Far North.

Bob himself had grown up near Bellingham, in a double-wide mobile home owned by an aunt. He never graduated from high school. He began cutting cedar bolts at fifteen and shipped out for Alaska two years later, while other boys his age were playing baseball.

The *Fearless* left Skagway with her quarters stocked with gear and her fuel tanks topped off with diesel oil. It was a bright, even joyous July day as they manoeuvred past Eldred Rock and Sullivan Island. While his boat made the run down Lynn Canal, Bob tuned the radar and depth sounder, and because the sun was out on a fair afternoon and the green Alaskan waters lay sleek and glassy, and because his new deckhand seemed stalwart and reliable he felt – for the first time since May – good about things.

Bob went outside, made his way forward, and peered up into the pilot-house window, where Paul – he would not forget this – stood tall behind the wheel. The boy nodded at him gravely, as though he had been steering the *Fearless* for many years – a black-haired boy with blue eyes and a clear face – then fixed his youthful gaze once again to the southeast and the promise of the Chatham Strait fishing grounds.

There was a net closure – no net fishing allowed – so for a few days they trolled for silvers. They worked the rip at

Point Gardner for a dozen modest fish; they dragged
twenty-two fathoms off Admiralty Island for two dozen
more. Bob showed Paul how to work the gurdies and
how to unsnap the leaders as they came up with their
spoons and how to coil them neatly in the stern. The boy
learned immediately how to gaff his fish behind the gills
so as to avoid damaging the meat. Then came a twenty-
four-hour gill-net opening. They fished a tight corner
with the Port Protection fleet, the tide running hard, the
boats close to one another, the evening westerly tossing
spray over the pilothouses. In the dark the boy picked his
first net clean – sixty-five good chums in a stiff night
wind beneath the season's first northern lights. The
moon went down and they fished the beach by radar,
running in tight and dropping the net light, then
ploughing out again and dropping net off the drum.
They drifted through a kelp bed and the boy cleaned out
the net, dropping fish in the hold and strands of kelp over
the side. Then, with the net set, they revealed themselves.

The boy had spoken about high-school football games
and of his painful seasons on the wrestling team. He
could play the guitar, he insisted; he had once played the
violin, too. He regretted his lack of a greater seriousness
when it came to making music. He had smoked
marijuana more than a few times but had taken LSD
only once – yes, their son had dropped acid, said Bob; it
was something he had to tell them. In the course of
Paul's acid trip he had put his face beside a beehive
without trepidation and had relaxed enough to climb a
sheer cliff and had wandered down the fairways of a golf
course. He was not sure if he wanted to go to college. He
thought perhaps that he would own a health club or
open a pizza parlour. Other times, he said, he wanted to

be a cop; maybe, then again maybe not. He confessed to confusion about his future and announced that during his time aboard he had come to miss the company of women. He wanted, he said, to be close to somebody, that much he knew.

The next day they struck surf scoters off the water, and the boy remembered duck hunting long ago and the eccentricities of his family's long-dead chocolate Lab, a timid dog named Duke.

In August Paul confronted his first evil weather. They set the net in a heavy rain, a big wind driving sea-water across both decks. A gale came up, the tide ebbed hard, and Bob decided to reel up and slip into a bight in the shoreline. But the high speed in the reel drive quit against the tide with two-thirds of the net still in the water. In the storm, with the wind blowing the tops off the waves and the offshore rips boiling in overfalls and combers, the *Fearless* towed her net beyond Cape Lynch, where the tide swept her out to open water. The net-winch clutch quit working after fifteen minutes, so the two of them pulled net by hand. They took turns. They worked in their rain gear with the sea coming from all directions, a maelstrom from which they turned their faces. Darkness came and the sea steepened; the *Fearless* cupped deeply into westerly swells and Bob had to stay behind the wheel. Paul pulled for four hours with the sea bellowing in his ears. It was what he'd come to Alaska for in the first place, Bob knew, what he believed in some deep private corner of his heart. *Tribulation and hardship.* Later Paul admitted to this. He said that his father had trained it into him.

Weather prevented them from making the run south, and for three days they lay at anchor at Twin Coves,

holed up and reading novels. Bob brought out his bag of
marijuana and they smoked a lot of it. The boy began to
speak out of boredom and recollected the high-school
girls he'd undressed and fondled and sometimes planked,
and then he communicated to Bob a recent revelation: If
you liked somebody, the sex was better. If you loved
somebody, it was like floating in marmalade clouds
heated five degrees above room temperature. If you
didn't like somebody, forget everything. This he hadn't
known in high school.

Paul explained how he'd stolen on a regular basis
whole cases of beer from delivery trucks. Before football
games he'd popped little white speed pills, and once he'd
snorted cocaine. He'd been hauled in for weaving at high
speed down boulevards and his father – did
Mr Hutchinson recollect? – had come to the precinct
station at three-thirty in the morning to collect him with
no small disgust. The boy had puked in his father's Buick.
His father had pulled over to the shoulder of the freeway
and barked him across the brows. Did Mr Hutchinson
remember this incident? Paul with vomit dribbling in
strings from his lips and a welt forming between his eyes?

The summer after graduation the boy had gone to the
mountains with a friend from the football team. They'd
gobbled peyote buttons, and Paul, in the woods, had
dreamed of green Alaskan waters. In Alaska, he told Bob,
he intended to find himself.

Now, in Alaska, stoned on the deck of Bob's fishing
boat, Paul turned enlightened and decided that the key
to his existence was not to end up like his father. 'A real
macho freak,' he'd said to Bob Pomeroy. 'It's probably
too late,' the boy had added.

This was the truth, Bob told Hutchinson. This was
how Paul had spoken.

Actually, Paul had professed to be rethinking everything about his existence. Football, for example, and wrestling – he had never enjoyed either one. Why had he done these things anyway? What was the point? Maybe he would study psychology and figure it all out. He had recently, he said, read a psychology book – *On the Development of the Human Personality*, by Dr Anton Friedman. Some of you, the book stated, was just what the sperm and egg decided and a lot of you was what happened before you were two. Some more was between two and thirteen. After that, the book said, you did what you had to do, you were a robot. Bob had read no psychology books and wondered if there couldn't be some path of escape from such a fated, miserable condition. Paul thought that perhaps it was in another psychology book, that there were some people who thought so, yes.

They got more stoned and became unintelligible, even to themselves.

For three days there were sixty-knot winds and twelve-foot seas, and the wipers froze solid and ice formed in the rigging. In a lull they made the run down to Point Horton, but the radar locked up, and they had to jog through a snow squall, making no progress for eleven hours. In Ketchikan they paired up with another boat, the *Wayfarer*, for the run across Dixon Entrance. After two days the southeast gale died down and they lit south, running for home, but ill weather blew hard down from the north, and the two boats soon lay at anchor in Customhouse Cove with snow freezing against the pilothouse windows. Once again the rigging iced up; the radio reported steepening seas and a fifty-five-knot gale. Then, after three days of this, the forecast called for clearing and the skippers of the two boats agreed to run for it.

At three in the morning Bob flicked on the radar and stared for a long time at the empty scope while Paul slept in the fo'c'sle. A rough squall passed through Customhouse Cove, and, in his rain gear, reluctantly, Bob went out to let slip a few more yards of anchor chain. At dawn they pushed off for Foggy Bay with the *Wayfarer* running to port and in radio contact; they cleared Mary Island and ploughed into the vast open just as the Coast Guard broadcast an emergency gale warning for the length of the northern coast. Bob radioed the *Wayfarer*, but since the seas in front of them were apparently calm she radioed back to say they ought to run for Foggy Bay at least. There was time, her skipper said, before the wind came up.

The *Fearless* fell in, quartering to stern, but the wind, a northerly, came in at seven-thirty. The water darkened. The tops of the swells blew off all around so that shreds of foam flew past. The seas grew tall and the two boats jogged in tandem to put their trolling poles down. The last of the flood came at eight-fifteen, and as the tide turned back against the wind the sea rolled even higher. It rolled over both decks of the *Fearless* easily, so that Bob had to send Paul down to pump clear the bilges. At the wheel, Bob negotiated swells out of the west at first, then from the south with the southwest chop and the tide race pushing on top. The waves pressed so hard against the windows that the glass sagged with their weight. Water poured in over the stern, filled the cockpit, then drained as the boat throttled uphill. Once, to port, Bob caught a glimpse of the *Wayfarer*, a third of her keel visible as she rode the waves. Then Paul stood beside him with a strand of vomit hanging from his mouth and an ashen, defeated face.

Bob had passed a few storms at the bilges himself, clearing the pump filters of their detritus, wedged in tight alongside the engine, listening to its scream and breathing the putrid odour of diesel fumes, old salmon, and musty wood. It was not long before a person inevitably had to vomit in that unlit and windowless hellhole. The storm shook the entire length of the boat, and as you lay on your belly her hull shuddered under you, and you prayed with your face to the vomity ribbing that she wouldn't go under while you were down there alone beside that slamming engine.

'You'd better get down there,' Bob said. 'We gotta have you hard pumping bilge.'

'I need air,' the boy said. 'A couple minutes' worth of air.'

He descended anyway, shame-faced, wiping his mouth. Darkness came. The seas steepened further. Water buried the bow to the cabin; they lost radio contact with the *Wayfarer*, but Bob could see her running lights as she mounted into a nearby wave, and he was glad of her presence in that great emptiness. He kept the *Fearless* diving deep into the troughs and throttled hard up the steepest hills of white water, listening to the engine change pitch. Then, in the darkness, the mast toppled and with it the radio antenna. Bob heard them go, a crash that coincided with a tremendous shudder throughout the length of the boat. The *Fearless* listed to starboard while her mast still hung on by its rigging.

The boy emerged topside again and looked fearfully at Bob. For a moment he seemed about to speak and he blinked – it was a question.

'Cut it loose,' Bob Pomeroy ordered. 'Cut the whole mast right loose.'

The boy blinked. 'Now?' he asked. 'OK.'

Paul went out with a flashlight and a hatchet. It was the last time Bob saw him, alive or dead. He wore his rain gear. He went without question. There was vomit hanging from his lip.

They were swamped by three big ones in succession. They rode low and the engine died. The *Fearless* turned broadside immediately and, helpless now, did a half-roll into the ocean. It seemed to Bob both sudden and inevitable; he had just enough time to drag back the door of the pilothouse and make a grab before the water hit him.

He stayed with the boat, clinging to a gunnel, and called, screamed for Paul. The boy, no doubt, was hung up in the rigging, which now lay submerged beneath the waves. Either that or he'd been swept overboard. Bob went on calling for him anyway.

He called for no more than half a minute. Then he stopped. He adjusted his grip and hung on, silent. The lights of the *Wayfarer* cut through the sleet; she came near, her skipper made some minor adjustments – tricky and deft given the boiling of the waves – and then her deckhand tossed out a life ring. He missed for two or three tries before the *Wayfarer* quartered in closer. Bob hung on. He was getting numb; his hands no longer felt anything. The life ring came his way again. There were two more tries, and then he grabbed it. He let go of the gunnel and held on to the life ring. Then he was under. He came up again. The deckhand pulled him to within ten feet of the pilothouse before a wave pitched Bob on to the *Wayfarer's* afterdeck, where he broke his nose against the net winch.

After Bob Pomeroy had gone away – after the dinner and the complicit mourning, after they had falsely healed one another, two men moving toward a tidy farewell – Hutchinson's daughter wept uncontrollably and Hutchinson's wife consoled her. They sat together in a paralysed embrace astride the dining-room table. His daughter blew her nose repeatedly into a napkin, and his wife urged her to indulge herself fully. 'Weep,' she said. 'Let it go, darling.'

In the kitchen Hutchinson meted out three fingers of bourbon and stood for a long time beside the sink, a hand laid atop his head. The image of his son with the flashlight and the hatchet became more vivid as he stood there. He exerted himself to see this more clearly – the boy in rain gear, saying nothing in the storm, vomit depending from his chin. There are things no father should imagine, he realised.

He sat by himself at the kitchen table. Laura came in bearing a photo album and showed him the portrait he'd taken of Paul with his first slain duck, seven years ago. Then she removed it from its plastic sleeve and passed it into his keeping.

'That little story of yours,' she said. 'Your little Paul-and-his-first-duck story, like he ever wanted to go hunting in the first place. Like he ever *needed* that.'

'I didn't want to be like my father either,' Hutchinson reminded her. 'My father was such a coward, Laura. I responded to that.'

'Don't blame this on your father,' Laura said.

'There's no point in blame,' replied Hutchinson.

'Yes, there is,' said Laura.

He couldn't sit with her. He left. He went upstairs and sat in Paul's bedroom and looked at the boy's collection of sports trophies. He'd started him hunting at eight years old, he recalled; Paul had worn two sweaters. Hutchinson had

lit the hand warmer for him, and the boy passed the day
sitting on a plastic bag in the blind and pointing whenever
ducks went overhead.

Paul squeezed his fingers against his ears whenever
the gun went off. His cheeks flushed the hue of apple
skins. He chewed on candy bars; traces of them lay
against the corners of his lips. For a half-hour he held
a dead mallard in his lap, inspecting its legs and feet.
He slept going home, then woke and slipped a piece
of bubble gum between his teeth. He leaned against
the car door, watching the sageland outside his
window and humming violin *études*. The boy took
violin lessons after school, a thing he seemed to
enjoy. But he quit eventually, and Laura blamed
Hutchinson.

When Paul was twelve Hutchinson put a shotgun in
his hands. They went out three times, and the boy took
his shots without establishing the proper lead. Hutchinson did not desist, however. The boy had fast reflexes
and only needed consistent prodding to develop his
marksmanship.

It was early in December when the boy got his first
kill. They drove in under some power lines at dawn,
mallards getting off the little feeder stream before them.
They parked and hauled their decoys out, and the boy
watched the dark surface of the pond. 'It's all ice,' he
said. 'It's iced over.'

'We'll break it out,' answered Hutchinson. 'It's thin
enough stuff. We can break it.'

They walked a half-mile, through rushes, to a point
of sedge, the boy following Duke, who wagged his
tail. Hutchinson kicked out the ice in his waders.
'Come on in here,' he said to Paul. 'Help me out. I
need a hand.'

The boy kicked at the ice. It came free in fractured slabs. They set out the decoys in the shape of a V, its point aimed into the wind.

'It's cold,' the boy said. 'My fingers.'

'It's perfect,' answered Hutchinson. 'Some wind. A little weather. It'll be the only pond around with open water.'

'My waders are leaking,' the boy informed him.

They waited for a while in the reeds together. The boy sat beside the dog. Ducks began to move. Hutchinson brought down two stray teal as they winged in low just behind the blind, and Duke ineptly retrieved both of them.

'My feet are frozen,' the boy said.

'I know,' said Hutchinson. 'Mine are frozen, too. Your feet get cold when you go hunting.'

Hutchinson watched a flight of mallards circle. When they began to pull away he called them back; he worked them judiciously. 'OK,' he said to Paul. 'Be ready now. They're turning. They're all yours, son. *Take* them.'

'My hands are frozen,' Paul whined. 'I can't get my safety off.'

'Damn!' said Hutchinson. 'Get ready!'

The boy at last fired three shots, missing all, and reloaded without saying anything.

'You were under them,' explained Hutchinson. 'Throw your elbow out more. Lead smoothly.'

'My fingers are frozen,' the boy answered.

In the afternoon the weather worsened. A whipping snow fell, and the wind blew harder from the north.

'Let's go,' the boy said. 'I can't feel my feet. I don't *like* going hunting anyway.'

Hutchinson counselled patience. 'Dusk,' he said.
'You'll get good shots at dusk. They won't flare off
then. They'll be looking for a place to set.'

'I'm freezing.'

'It doesn't help to talk about it.'

'I can't feel my feet.'

'Me neither,' said Hutchinson. 'Just ignore it.'

The boy fell grimly quiet after this. He watched the
sky with his hands in his pockets, jumping up and down
in place, the gun on the ground beside him.

The snow landed on the shoulders of their coats now
and settled on their caps and on the decoys. The wind
blew it stinging into their faces. Flights of ducks would
appear in it suddenly, the whistling of their wings and
their cries long preceding them. It was fast shooting, and
Hutchinson felt challenged by it. By two-thirty he'd shot
his limit.

At three o'clock a single greenhead came winging low
across the point of sedge and Paul fired straight-on, and
then going-over and finally going-away. On the last shot
the duck arced steeply to the ice, where it flopped for a
while before settling.

'I hit him,' the boy said. But he didn't seem happy
about it, he seemed glum. He looked across the ice at the
place where the duck had fallen.

'Congratulations,' said Hutchinson. 'You've gotten
started.'

Duke would not venture out on to the ice, so
Hutchinson kicked a path directly through it and made
the retrieve himself.

They walked back to the truck and ran the heater.
Already Hutchinson was inventing the story of it: a long
third shot, the steep drop of the lone mallard, the boy too
astonished to say anything – too astonished to speak!

Hutchinson, just before dusk, made the boy stand beside the truck tailgate with his first duck clutched in his right fist. He brought his camera up to his face and peered at his son through the viewfinder. 'Smile, damn it,' he said to his son. 'That's your first duck you've got there.'

'I feel bad about killing him,' the boy said.

'I know,' said Hutchinson. 'Smile anyway.'

The boy tried. He'd felt an urge to please, that was clear now. That was too clear. His face contorted this way and that, searching for an appropriate configuration, until at last it arranged itself in the shape of a smile that was the falsest thing Hutchinson had ever seen.

'Come on,' he said. 'You don't look like yourself. Smile naturally, Paul.'

But it didn't happen, and Hutchinson was forced to snap the picture with his son's face arranged in this false way. *Look*, said the picture now, *I'm not myself. I only want to please.*

Remorse rolled through Hutchinson with all the force of an ocean wave. He knew that Paul's brief life had, in some measure, been a lie and that his death was Hutchinson's own to contend with; the son's death was on his father's hands.

Hutchinson's daughter was drinking vanilla cream tea and had the television on. It was one in the morning. Rain ricocheted off the windows. His daughter wore no make-up, she'd dropped her shoes on the rug. She was sadly overweight, and it caused him to wonder: what had made it thus? What cords connected to which ancestors? He understood that he didn't know the answer to this question. He was cognisant of his wider ignorance and of the mystery of his daughter. Perhaps he had never known her. Perhaps she was troubled in a private way, or loathed him secretly.

He touched her cheek, and then her chin, and then he kissed the top of her head. 'I'm sorry,' he said. 'I'm so sorry, Cara.'

'Go see Mom,' his daughter answered.

He went to Laura in the bedroom. She was in bed, and she did not turn toward him at first when he sat down at the foot of the mattress. 'My God,' she said. 'I keep thinking of it. Seeing him underwater like that. It's just . . . my God,' she repeated.

'Laura,' he said. 'Please look at me.'

'I can't stand to think of it,' Laura told him. 'All of it, none of it, it's just so – '

She wept.

'Laura,' he said. 'Forgive me.'

'Forgiveness is hard,' his wife whispered hoarsely. 'It isn't in me, you know.'

'You've been right about everything,' explained Hutchinson. 'I'm guilty, guilty, I've – '

She held him then, but with a distant pity, and they were both inconsolable.

'What was it I ever loved in you?' his wife said after a while. 'Why in God's name did I love you?'

'I don't know,' Hutchinson cried. 'How can I answer that?'

But after ten minutes she held him tightly and cradled his head in her hands. He felt, now, that her sadness included him. 'Calm yourself,' she whispered, and Hutchinson was as grateful for that as he had ever been for anything in all of his fifty years. 'Quiet now,' she breathed. 'Peace, peace and quiet.'

That night his erection was powerful, bursting with his sadness. Afterward he cried with his face in her greying hair. They lay side by side looking up at the ceiling. 'What the hell is everything about?' he said. 'None of it makes any sense.'

'You're human,' she replied. 'You're frail.'

He put his head against her belly, in the warm place he had been accustomed to in the days before his son drowned.

The Queen and I
Jay McInerney

As the tired light drains into the Western suburbs beyond
the river, the rotting pier at the end of Gansevoort Street
begins to shudder and groan with life. From inside a
tinroofed warehouse, human beings stagger out into the
steamy dusk like bats leaving their cave. Inside the shed
one can make out in the dimness a sprawling white
mountain, the slopes of which are patched with sleeping
bags, mattresses, blankets, cardboard and rafts of
plywood. An implausible rumour circulates among the
inhabitants of this place that the white mesa is made of
salt which was once, when there were still funds for
municipal services, spread on the icy city streets in
winter; at present the rusting warehouse serves as a
huge dormitory and rat ranch. At dusk the inmates rise
to work, crawling out into the last light to dress and
make-up. Down on the edge of the highway along the
foot of the pier, the shiny cars of pimps and johns wait
alongside the beat-up vans from the rescue missions and
religious organisations, ready to compete for the bodies
and souls of the pierdwellers.

Covering the waterfront, I watch as three queens share
a mirror and a lipstick, blinking in the slanted light
outside the shed which houses the mountain of salt.
One of them steps away a few feet, creating a symbolic
privacy in which to pull up his skirt demurely and take a
torrential leak. A second lights up a cigarette and tugs on

a pair of fishnet hose. The third is my friend Marilyn, queen of Little West 12th Street. It's my first night on the job.

I ran into Marilyn in the emergency room at Saint Vincent's a couple of days before. I went in for gingivitis, my gums bleeding and disappearing up the sides of my teeth from bad nutrition and bad drugs. It's a common street affliction, another credential in my downward slide toward authenticity. Marilyn had a broken nose, three cracked ribs and assorted bruises from a trick who had second thoughts.

'I thought you had a pimp, Marilyn,' I said, watching a gunshot victim bleed on a gurney.

'The pimp, he get killed by the Colombians,' said Marilyn. 'He never protect me anyways, the bastard. He punch me hisself.' Marilyn laughed through his nose, then winced with pain. When he could speak again he said, 'Last time my nose is broken it's my papa do the breaking. He beat the shit out me when he find me dressed in Mama's wedding gown. I'm holding the lipstick and he opens the door of my room. Smack me good, scream at me, call me a dirty little maricon, he don't want no maricon for a son. The boy last night, he was like that, this big bulging muscle New Chursey boy. After I do him, he start hitting, calling me faggot. A lot them like that, they don't like what they want. Hey, man,' he said, scrutinising me with new interest. 'Why don't you be my pimp? I give you five dollar on every trick.'

It was a measure of my prospects that I thought it was a pretty good offer. In fact, I'd been similarly unemployed by a recent murder and was sleeping in Abingdon Square Park. I was dealing halves and quarters of coke out of a bar on 13th when my man got whacked and I was left without a connection. Before that I'd been in a band but the drummer ODed and the bassist moved to LA.

When I first met Marilyn I was living in a cellar in the meat district. Marilyn worked all night, and I was awake jonesing on coke or crack and trying to write. I am a songwriter, you see, a poet Mo-dee. There is beautiful, ugly music inside me, which plays in the performance space deep in my mind. Walking the streets, doing the bars, I hear snatches of it in the distance, above the subliminal bass line of the urban heartbeat. I am most attuned to it in moments of transport, when I'm loaded on cheap wine or crack. Sometimes I'm dead certain that one more drink, one more hit and I will grasp its essence and carry it back with me to the other side. A student of lowlife, zoologist of artifice and aesthetician of ugliness, I am living here in the gutter like Prince Hal, biding my time, waiting to burst forth like a goddamned sun.

A refugee from the western suburbs, I used to skip school and take the bus into the city. I hung out on St Mark's Place and the Bowery, copping the look and the attitude of punk, discovering Bukowski and the Beats in the book shops. Returning to the subdivisions of Jersey was an embarrassment. The soil was too thin for art. No poetry could ever grow in the grapefruit rinds of the compost heap. Ashamed of my origins, neither high nor low, I dreamed of smoky bars and cafés, steaming slums. I wanted to get down and dirty. I believed that the lowest road would lead me to the height of consciousness, that to conceive beauty it was necessary to sleep with ugliness. I've been in that bed for several years now. So far nobody's knocked up.

Like Dylan says – Someday everything is gonna be different, when I paint my masterpiece. I will be rich and famous and photographed with models who will suddenly find me incredibly attractive – my goodness, where have I been all their short naughty long-legged lives? – and I will do a lot of expensive designer drugs and behave very badly and ruin my promising career and end up right back here in the gutter. And I'll wish I'd been good to the people I met on the way up because they'll piss all over me when I meet them again on the way down. And I'll write a song cycle about it. It'll be excellently poignant, even tragic.

Marilyn grew up in Spanish Harlem, where he was christened with the name Jesus, a delicate boy with a sweet face who is plausibly a piece of ass as a girl. He wants to get married and live the kind of life I grew up in. Except he wants to do it as a woman. At night he looks longingly out over the Hudson at the dim glow of suburban New Jersey the way I used to look over from the other side at the lights of Manhattan. He wants a three-bedroom house in the burbs which he can clean and polish while he waits for a husband who works in the city. There's a huge Maxwell House sign across the river from the Gansevoort pier, and he told me once that when he wakes up as the average American workday is ending he remembers the tuneful Maxwell House ads he saw when he was a kid, dreaming about being the perky wife percolating a pot of coffee for sleepy hubby.

The doctor who gives Marilyn his hormone shots says that more than half of the – what shall we call them? – people who get the operation get married, and that more than half of those who do don't tell their husbands about their former lives as men. I personally find this just a teensy bit hard to believe. But Marilyn believes and he's saving up to pay for the operation.

Poor Marilyn with his broken snout. In his business he needs to be able to breathe through his nose. I

decide to give it a shot. Could be a song in it. Plus I'm
stone broke.

So as the sun goes down beyond the river into the
middle of America where the cows are coming home to
their barns and guys with lunchboxes and briefcases are
dragging ass home to their wives I am trudging toward
the meat district with Marilyn, who is wearing fishnet
hose under a green vinyl miniskirt and a loose black top.
The Queen and I.

'How I look, honey?' Marilyn asks.

'Looking bad, looking good,' I say.

'This my Madonna look. Those Jersey boys – they
love it.'

By now I'm sure you've guessed that Marilyn is
currently a blonde.

The smell gets worse as we approach Washington and
Gansevoort, which is Marilyn's beat – the warehouses
full of dead meat, the prevailing smell of rot inextricably
linked in my mind with the stench of urine and
excrement and spent semen. A sign says 'VEAL SPECIA-
LISTS: HOT HOUSE BABY LAMBS, SUCKLING PIGS & KID
GOATS'. Whoa! Sounds like that shit should be illegal,
you know what I'm saying?

With darkness falling on the meat-packing district a
slow and funky metamorphosis is taking place. Refri-
gerated trucks haul away from loading docks while
rough men in bloody aprons yank down metal shutters
and padlock sliding doors. The suffocating smell of
rotting meat hangs over the neighbourhood, and, when
the breeze blows east of the Hudson, infiltrates the smug
apartments and cafés of Greenwich Village – which is the
only good thing I can say about this stench.

As the trucks disappear toward New Jersey and
upstate, strange creatures materialise on the broken

sidewalks as if spontaneously generated from the rotting flesh. Poised on high heels, undulant with the exaggerated shimmy of courtship – a race of lanky stylised bipeds commands the street corners. They thrust lips and hips at passing cars, those cars that pass this time of night, the area not exactly being on the direct route to anything except Hell or Hoboken. Passenger wheels that find their way here cruise slowly down the unlit cobbled streets, circling and returning to pass the sidewalk sirens. Sometimes a car slows to a stop near one of the posing figures who leans over the driver's window to consult, haggle and flirt, sometimes to walk around the car and slip inside the passenger door, disappearing to reappear a few minutes later.

The sirens of Washington Street come in all sizes, colours and nose shapes and in this light not all of them are hard to look at. One lifts a halter top to expose a lunar pair of taut white breasts as a red Toyota with Connecticut plates crawls past. It's just barely conceivable that some of these sports in the cars who transact for five minutes of sex believe that they're getting it straight. But ladies, I wouldn't count on it. I mean if it's your fiancé gets busted down here you might think about cancelling the band and the tent and the cake. Or maybe not. They're probably good family men, most of them. And so long as clothes and make-up stay in place no one needs to start parsing his proclivities and worrying about whether he's straight. Sometimes the cops sweep through to meet arrest quotas; johns who find their pleasure interrupted by a sudden official rap on the car window almost always act shocked when the cops expose the gender of their sexual partners with a playful tug of the waistband or the not-so-playful rending of a skirt.

The clientele is nothing if not diverse, arriving in limos and Chevies, Jags and Toyotas. Whenever a certain homophobic movie star is visiting New York – a comic renowned for obscene stand-up routines which outrage the gay and feminist communities, his white stretch limousine is bound to appear on Washington Street in the small hours of the morning and to linger there.

I take up a post beneath a sagging metal awning, half-concealed in the shadows, while Marilyn takes out his compact to check on the goods. He frowns. 'That salt, is terrible for my skin. Suck the moisture right out, sleeping every night on a big pile of salt. Even the rats don't like to live on the salt.' Is that because the rats are worried about their complexions? I wonder. Meantime Marilyn strikes a pose he has borrowed from a Madonna video near the kerb.

Just up the street is Randi, who claims he used to play with the Harlem Globetrotters. Wearing a leather mini and a red halter, Randi stands six foot eight in heels beneath a sign that says FRANKS SALAMI BOLOGNA LIVERWURST KNOCKWURST STEW MEATS & SKIRT STEAKS. Truth in advertising.

Down Gansevoort at the edge of the district the neon sign of a fashionable diner emits a pink glow. So very far away – this place where the assholes I went to college with are tossing back parti-coloured drinks and discussing the stock market and interoffice gropings and penetrations. Like my former best friend George Cribbs who wanted to be a poet and works for an ad agency in midtown. We roomed together at NYU, which I attended for two years and dropped out of because I was way too cool. After George graduated we'd meet for drinks at the Lion's Head or the White Horse Tavern where he thought he was slumming and I felt like an interloper among the gentry. So excited when he first walked in as a freshman with a fake ID from a store on 42nd Street that Dylan Thomas had practically died where we were sitting, but gradually, over the years, he decided that the Welsh bard had wasted and abused his talent. I mean, sure, George admitted, he was great, but what was the matter with being comfortable, taking care of your health, eating sensibly and writing copy for Procter and Gamble in between cranking out those lyrical heart's cries. And I'm on my best behaviour nodding like an idiot coming down off something I smoked or snorted and hoping the bartender won't remember he threw me out three months before. And gradually I think it became too embarrassing for both of us. I stopped calling and Lord knows I don't have a phone, except maybe the open-air unit on the corner of Hudson and 12th. Actually, it's been a relief to quit pretending.

Farther down Washington Street a trio of junkies build a fire in a garbage can, although the night is hot and steamy – the heat of the day, stored up in the concrete and asphalt, coming off now, cooking every-one slowly like so much meat. These old guys, after they been on the street a few years they never really get warm again. The winter cold stays with you in your bones through the long stinking summer and for ever, like a scar. The old farts who wear overcoats and boots in August. Plus that way you don't have to change your clothes for winter. One style fits all. I'm just fine in my black T-shirt and denim jacket which doubles as a blanket, thanks. Be off the street before that happens to me. When I paint my masterpiece. Franks salami bologna.

A red Nissan Z slows to a stop. Marilyn sashays over to
the car and schmoozes the driver, turns and waves to me.
I come out of the shadow to reveal myself in all my
freaky emaciated menace, moon-white face and dyed
black hair, my yellow teeth in their bleedy gums.
Marilyn zips around to the passenger side and climbs
into the Z, which makes the right and slows to a stop half
a block down the street where I can still see it. A bum in
an overcoat parks his overflowing shopping cart on the
sidewalk and peers in the window at the brightly lit
diners eating steak frites.

Eventually Marilyn comes back from his date, adjust-
ing his clothes and checking his make-up in a compact,
like a model. That's what he calls it – a date. He hands
me a damp, crumpled fiver. I don't want to think about
the dampness at all. I want to scrape the bill off my palm
and throw it into the stinking street, but Marilyn's all
excited about being back at work and planning for the
future. He's talking about how it will be after the
operation, after he gets married and moves to New
Chursey and I want to slap him and tell him that it's
the land of the living dead. It's not real, like this fabulous
life we're living here on Gansevoort Street with its franks
salami and bologna. The flesh they grill on their Webers
out in Morristown comes out of these very malodorous
warehouses against which we bravely slouch.

At least Marilyn will be spared the ordeal of having a
rotten suburban brat who will grow up to resent and
despise him for being a boring submissive suburban
housewife.

As the night deepens business picks up and I become
nearly accustomed to the layered stench, the several
octaves of decay. The old men sharing a bottle around
the fire pass out and the fire dies. I skulk over to Hudson

and buy myself a bottle of blackberry brandy to keep my motor running. A dealer strolls by offering coke, crack and smoke. At first I think no, I'm on duty, but the second time he comes by I have twenty dollars in my pocket from Marilyn and I buy a little rock and fire it up, tickling my brain, making me feel righteous and empowered – I'm here, I'm cool, I'm feeling so good, I'm going to be all right, the future is mine and I'm back on my feet and if I can just smoke a little more of this I'll keep feeling this way instead of slipping back, just a little more to maintain, to stop this fading, to stop this falling away from the perfect moment that was here just a minute ago, to hear that perfect tune in the deep of my brain, that masterpiece.

Franks bologna etcetera.

The buzz has slipped away like a heartbreakingly hot girl at a bar who said she'd be right back in a minute, promise. Leaving me oh so very sad and cranky. Where is the goddamn dealer?

The traffic in and out of the diner picks up around four when the clubs close, yellow cabs pulling up to dispense black-clad party people like Pez, the hip young boys and girls who are not yet ready for bed. I buy a so-called quarter of alleged toot and snort it all at once thinking it will carry me further, slower than smoking rocks.

Marilyn gets eleven dates for the night, a cavalcade of perverts representing several states, classes and ethnic groups, including a Hasid jeweller with the long slinky forelocks that bounce up and down as he bucks to fulfilment in the front seat of his black Lincoln, a construction worker with Jersey plates in a Subaru still wearing his hardhat and a stretch limo where the guy tells Marilyn he's in the movie business and tips twenty.

The Lambs of God van cruises up, pulls over beside us. The priest says, 'Top of the morning, Marilyn.' He looks surprised, not necessarily happy, when I slink out of my vampire shadow.

'Hello, Father,' says Marilyn. 'You looking for me tonight?'

'No, no, just checking to see that you're not . . . needing . . . anything.'

'Fine thanks, Father. And you?'

'Bless you and be careful, my child.' The priest guns the engine and pulls away.

'Very nice, the Father, but shy,' says Marilyn, a note of disappointment in his voice. 'I think maybe you scare him off.'

'The shy shepherd,' I say.

'I stay at that Lamb of God shelter one night and he didn't ask me for nothing,' says Marilyn, as if this were a heroic feat of selfless ministry. 'That day he just cop a little squeeze when I'm leaving. Food pretty decent, too.' We watch a car go by, slowly, the driver looking us over from behind his sunglasses. He seemed about to stop, then he peeled out and tore down the street. After a long pause, Marilyn said, 'My very first date was a priest, when I was an altar boy. He give me some wine.'

'Sounds very romantic,' I say, recalling that I was an altar boy once in another life. I was in awe of my proximity to the sacred rituals. I didn't smoke or swear and I confessed my impure thoughts to the eager priest behind the screen until the day my thoughts transmuted themselves to deeds on Mary Lynch's couch one afternoon, which I failed to mention at my next confession, suffering the guilt of the damned as I slunk away from the confessional booth. When lightning failed to strike me through the days and weeks that followed I began to resent my guilt and then to resent the faith that was so at odds with my secret nature and to exult in my rebellion. And as I turned away from my parents and church I created my own cult to venerate the taboo. Which perverse faith I am stubbornly observing here at five in the morning at the corner of Gansevoort and Washington.

Another car cruises by slowly, a junkyard Buick with two guys in the front seat. The twos are potentially dangerous so I decide I'll show my flag, talk to them myself. I tell Marilyn to stay put and saunter over to the car. The driver has to open the door because the window doesn't roll down. Two small Hispanic men in their fifties. 'Twenty apiece,' I say, nodding toward Marilyn. 'And you stay on this block.' Finally we agree on thirty-five for two.

I wave Marilyn over and he climbs in the back seat and I'm just leaning back against the building lighting a smoke when Marilyn comes howling and tumbling out of the car, crawling furiously as the car peels out, tyres squealing on the cobblestones. Marilyn flings himself on me and I hold him as he sobs. '*Es mi padre*,' he wails, '*mi padre*.'

'A priest?' I query, hopefully.

He shakes his head violently against my shoulder and suddenly he raises his face and starts apologising for getting make-up on me, wiping at my shoulder, apologising about my jacket, still crying. 'I ruin your jacket,' he says, crying hysterically. It's all I can do to convince him that I don't give a shit about the jacket which started out filthy anyway.

'Are you sure it was . . . him?' I ask.

Gulping air, he nods vehemently. He is sobbing and shaking, and I'm more than a little freaked out myself. I mean, Jesus.

Finally when he has calmed down I suggest we call it a
night. 'It's the first time I see him in three years,' Marilyn
says. I make him drink the rest of the blackberry brandy
and walk him back to the dock in the grainy grey light.
As the sun comes up behind us we stand on the edge of
the pier and look out over the river at the Maxwell
House sign. I can't think of anything to say. I put my arm
around him and he sniffles on my shoulder. From a
distance we would look like any other couple, I think.
Finally I suggest he get some sleep and he picks his way
across the rotting boards back to the salt mountain. And
that's the end of my career as a pimp.

A year after this happened I went back to look for
Marilyn. Most of the girls on the street were new to me,
but I found Randi, the former Globetrotter, who at first
didn't remember me. I do look different now. He
thought I was a cop, and then he thought I was a
reporter. He wanted money to talk, and finally I gave
him ten and he said, 'I remember you, you was that
crackhead.' Nice to be remembered. I asked if he had
seen Marilyn and he said Marilyn had disappeared
suddenly – 'maybe like, I don't know, seems like a year
ago'. He couldn't tell me anything and he didn't want to
know.

About a year after that I spotted a wedding announce-
ment in the *Times*. I admit I'd been checking all that time
– perusing what we once called the Women's Sports
pages – like an idiot, occasionally rewarded with the
picture of a high-school or college acquaintance, and
then one fine morning I saw a picture that stopped me.
Actually, I think I noticed the name first – otherwise I
might not have stopped at the picture. Marilyn Bergdorf
to wed Ronald Dubowski. It would be just like Marilyn

to name himself after a chic department store. I stared at the photo for a long time, and though I wouldn't swear to it in a murder trial I think it was my Marilyn – surgically altered, one presumes – that married Ronald Dubowski, orthodontist, of Oyster Bay, Long Island. I suppose I could have called, but I didn't.

So I don't really know how that night affected Marilyn, if it changed his life, if he is officially and anatomically a woman, now, or even if he is alive. I do know that lives can change overnight, though it usually takes much longer than that to comprehend that it has happened, to sense that we have changed direction. A week after Marilyn almost had sex with his father I checked myself into Phoenix House. I called my parents for the first time in more than a year. Now, two years later, I have a boring job and a crummy apartment and a girlfriend who makes the rest of it seem almost OK. I'd be lying if I said there aren't times I miss the old days, or that I don't breathe a huge sigh of relief when I climb on the train after a few hours spent visiting my parents, or that it's a gas being straight all the time, but still I'm grateful to be where I am now.

You think you're living a secret and temporary life, underground, in the dark. You don't imagine that someone will drive up the street, or walk in the door or look through the window – someone who will reveal you to yourself not as you hope to be in some glorious future metamorphosis but as you find yourself at that moment. Whatever you are doing then, you will have to stop and say, 'Yes, this is me.'

Change of Use
Candia McWilliam

In the pantry at the back of the long house, Mary shifted
back a little on the edge of the stone sink, as she had done
since these Thursday rituals began. She wanted to
balance so she could drift off into her own thoughts
without falling in or letting Mr Charteris know that she
was not fully with him as he pushed away at her with his
hands wringing one another on the rattling taps behind
her back. She had given him green beans for lunch for a
change, instead of peas with the Thursday shepherd's pie.
She could smell the blackberry and apple she was making
for his dinner cooking away under its crumble in the low
oven.

'Tell me your name again, my dear,' said Mr Charteris.

'Dorothy,' said Mary, to liven things up.

Overwhelmed by this unanticipated new companion,
Mr Charteris shook sadly as though to rid himself of
dust, buttoned, sighed, pushed Mary aside like a curtain
and washed his hands under taps that quivered as the
water promised to arrive, held off and then gushed out,
hot and chalky, through the aged piping into the sink
where tonight's potatoes eyed him smugly from the
colander.

He dried his hands while Mary set the kettle to boil.
Upstairs the house slept, as it would for another twenty-
five minutes.

He felt astonishingly well, astonishingly.

He smelt the tea as she spooned it from the red-and-gold caddy, saw her skin it seemed to him glow with the new life Thursdays must bring her, felt the sunshine as it came in slabs through the barred deep windows of the back of the house that looked on to lawn and shrubs and finally thicket, copse and wood. No one knew the house as he did. He had been a boy here and would die here. Each room held its story for him.

Mr Charteris sat down and rested his forearms on the kitchen table.

Mary brought him a tray of old silver, some cloths and the tin of polish.

'The lid's hard,' said Mr Charteris. 'Got stuck. When it dries this stuff's like glue.'

'I'm sure you can do it,' said Mary, pouring water on to the tea leaves from the heavy kettle off the stove. She kicked herself for not having tested the lid of the polish tin. This part was as important for him as what had gone before. She was sure that these Thursdays didn't take life from him but put it back. Maybe the care she was offering him was not orthodox, but it was natural.

'There. Done it. Nothing like experience,' said Mr Charteris.

She hoped he wouldn't look too closely at the silver on the tray. Not much of it matched and not all of it was silver. She'd brought some deliberately for him from other places she worked at.

'This tea's just the thing,' said Mr Charteris. 'Polishing dries out the tubes.'

She looked over at him from the lower oven where she was testing the crumble with a spoon. Her overall was getting tight. She shut the heavy door and bathed in the heat of butter and sugar burning together. It all made her hungry, she couldn't help it. She was hungry all the time now.

'Yes, and that is thirsty work too,' said Mr Charteris, supposing he should now pat Mary's bottom to go with the words, but not bothering to get up and go over to her actually to do this, because now came the reliable pleasure of his afternoon, the creaming and dipping and rubbing and the revelation of the silver. The distinction between his younger days and these later years was this for him: then he had been blind to the beauty of habit; now it was a luxury, a conscious indulgence as irresistible as yawning, stretching, surrendering to sleep.

Habit had become his bride, his chosen ravishment, his companion elect. It was simply that his wish to share his habit with just one other person at a time was not encouraged by the new masters here.

Mary was wondering how to keep the room empty for long enough to let Mr Charteris be through with his polishing. She relied upon the herd instinct, the set of rules that kept the rest of the residents of the house hung about their routine like a beard of bees.

He was holding up each knife to the light, checking each fork for speckles of erosion, the bruise of tarnish. To the left of the tray on the silver cloth he set the cleaned utensils, to the right lay the unpolished. The whole collection shone about as much as a dish of sardines and vinegar on toast. Still it made him so glad that she guessed he saw a shine not visible to her.

She heard the stomp and waltz of the polishing machine start up on the ballroom floor above. Along the kitchen ceiling ran wiring and pipes that made abrupt changes of direction. From hooks along the wall hung clutches of keys. A plastic fire extinguisher in a glass case sat above its predecessor, a heavy metal torpedo that said on its side 'Last Date of Service: June 1956'.

She heard a rustle in the pantry.

In there, the baleful wedges of wholesale cheese lay plastic-sealed and piled on the slate shelf. Mary reached in her hand behind one and pulled out the humane mousetrap. The creature inside flustered between its perspex chambers.

How humane was it to take the humane mousetrap to the outhouse where the cats had their hideout? She carried the fretful snack and tipped it out in front of the cat she considered to be the idlest. That way, it was fairer.

Two slow frivolous bats of its paw later, the cat was happily prolonging this small local torment.

From the back door, the kitchen looked as it could have almost any Thursday afternoon of the century as Mr Charteris had by now often described it to her.

Mr Charteris polished away, his apron black, his extensible cuff-restrainers glistening, the cup of tea neglected. His hair was white as salt, his face of a kind that is no longer trained into being – unremarkable features withheld by years of emulative mimicry into an expression of checked emotion and impersonal superiority. But his eyes were a disturbingly self-willed brown, where one might have expected self-effacing blue.

Looking out from the other kitchen door facing the gates at the front of the house and up the outer stairway to the terrace, Mary saw today's afternoon beginning. Two of the older ladies were wheeled out, a sunshade set above them, a tea tray brought. No bell had woken the after-lunch sleepers, but the windows began to show movement behind themselves; a few blinds were raised. In the main rooms, between the grave, flattened, central columns of the pediment, there was the sound of dance music, a raised voice, an insistent hard tapping.

Among the trees on the lawn, figures dressed just like Mary moved between chairs and benches, recliners covered with rugs where still bodies lay, stirring them, sometimes with a word, sometimes a touch. They seemed to be competing with one another to awaken a sleeper. Over some of the bodies, the overalled men and women shrugged vehemently, like cricketers loosening up. It was as though there were two teams, one ghoulishly dedicated to fun and activity, the other to repose. In the wide green of the afternoon, somnolence had the worst of it for the time being but could well show form later. The classical enclosure of the park suggested an eventual triumph of sleep.

The gates in front of the house's wide face implied a fixed modesty that must prevail in the end. The house would shut itself away, a fading beauty needing sleep in order to reawaken refreshed.

Driving the laundry van in at the gates, Francis Mullard changed down at the turning off the main road, felt the cattle grid under the wheels, slowed again on turning into the asphalted back drive, and wondered if the grid kept the old folks in, too. In the back of the van the sheets were cold and heavy inside the hampers. The van had been parked in the underground car-park of the laundry, where it never got warm, even in a summer like this one.

Francis's own grandmother was living at home with them at present. Her very active ways had knocked them for six at first, but now they were used to her walking miles in the night over their heads and bringing alarmed or desperate or boring strangers back to the house from her random samplings of different places and acts of worship.

Gran had forced Francis and Pat to get out much more.

They could not endure her pity at the start of their rare coincidental weekends off, when they were prepared to settle in to two days of doing nothing much, and she ran them through her commitments. She was a freelance indexer of historical works, and a self-appointed tidier of graves and churches, so the kitchen and living room were convenient spaces for setting out the details of a reign, a battle, a marriage or a plot.

The rubbish bin and waste-paper baskets overflowed with the things Francis's grandmother had found unfitting in church or cemetery, gloves or cans or inspirational paperbacks, silver-paper horseshoes and ballpoint pens.

'Don't put down that pot!' Gran shrieked to Pat, as he tried to fetch Francis's tea in the morning. 'You could unsettle the Anabaptists!'

While they were out at work, Pat at the restaurant and Francis driving the laundry around, Gran covered any space there was with $3 \times 5''$ index cards and blue post-its. Both Francis and Pat worked shifts, so they never knew if the other had even attempted to release some space from the formation of battle at Oudenarde, the machinations of the Cabal or Ironbridge Telford's gazetted surviving works. When they got in they either fetched something to eat and took it up to bed, or rushed out, feeling illicit and safe. Very rarely, they shared a precarious feast with Francis's grandmother.

In a way, Gran had brought back the cramped romantic first days of their love, when they had nothing to hide because no one would have believed even if they'd written it out loud all over the bathroom mirror. They were such good friends, friends from their per-ambulators, more like brothers. This was the line still adopted by Francis's mother, Kay, who hoovered between the feet of her husband as he sat in his chair, and always baked double to freeze half in case of sudden guests.

It was fortunate that Francis had always loved Pat, since there'd been no sudden guest, ever, within a cherry's spit of their house.

Sometimes at night Pat would make a meal for Francis and Gran, picking his way between the bits of information on paper and the birds' nests of ecclesiastical leavings. He would recreate what he had served in the restaurant earlier. Although he wasn't yet a chef, he had the curiosity and steady hands for it; he worked so hard it was really only a matter of time before he got the promotion. He was at the stage now when you did the one thing over and over till you could do it in your sleep – if you got any, that was. It seemed oddly miniature to him to concoct meals just for Francis and his grandmother, an eccentric hobby nothing much to do with work. Himself, he ate through the pores all day and could barely stand food at the end of it. He ate smoke and drank water. When he saw Francis's thickening waist, he was proud of it.

'I made that,' he'd say to Gran, who would reply, 'Much to be proud of there,' and join Pat outside the lean-to for a cig after whatever rich meal the boy had made.

All very comfortable, until just recently, when Kay had started on about the calls she was getting from dissatisfied authors.

'They say Mother's having them on. Either that, or she's losing her accuracy,' she said to Pat, whom she'd rung at the restaurant, sure of getting a better hearing than she would from her own son. 'You can't do work for other people and be inaccurate. They plain don't like it. It shows them up.'

'Perhaps she means to,' said Pat, which was no more than what he thought.

'She's always been scrupulous about her research. She even stores her thoughts alphabetically. If you ask about the car you don't have to wait as long as if you ask her about Francis. And if I ask about you there's a slightly longer wait while she locates P.'

'She's maybe tired of sorting other people's words.'

'If you like it, it's not the sort of thing you go off,' said Kay. 'I should know, I've never cared a fig for it and still don't.'

Since she was not Pat's mother, he was not as irked by her angle as Francis would have been.

He approached Francis.

'Do you think your grandmother's losing it?' he asked.

'Nope. She may have a project on, though.' Francis had walked back from the depot where he had left the van. He was determined to do something about it before he had to change his waist size for good. He'd give Pat a surprise.

'Try one of these. Red pepper straws. A bit of Gruyère and several dozen eggs.' Pat had made them specially, but pretended he'd brought them from work. Gran was upstairs working on an overcrowded letter 'V' in a work on the history of lenses and their effect on art history, whose author was at that moment enjoying some of Pat's cheese straws brought home by his wife in her handbag, after a business lunch.

'What type of project?' asked Pat.

'I think she's trying to get sent to a home.'

'No one does that. It's lonely, and it costs all you've got, no matter how much you've got. The body only gives out when it's cried all it can and spent all there is.'

'*You* say that,' said Francis, kissing him. 'But I think she's being tactful. That's why my mother's so tactless she could perform amputations with her afterthoughts. Because *her* mother's so tactful she makes everyone believe she's the one at fault, not them.'

'But no one wants to go into a home. Have you seen inside one? Home is what they're not. They can't call them what they are. Asylum is a lovely word in every way compared with what they are.'

'Maybe she's got some idea of going to a place where she can think it all out and then just lie down and float off. *I* don't know.'

'Bed's that place,' said Pat, who hated being alone and could not sort through his memories for very long without meeting Francis there, and fearing the day when they would not be within reach of one another.

'And move! And bend! And stretch!' sang the voice at the centre of the house, unsexed as a parrot. Mary walked up the right flank of the outside staircase up to the façade and looked in through the ballroom window.

Accompanied by a piano, the old men and women in nightwear or loose combinations of cotton followed the gestures of the strong fit body, wielding a smart black cane, that called to them. In their movements they gave hints of what they saw, like quiet flightless birds. They did not dance or exercise so much as talk with their hands, their necks, their knees, remembering longer, more abandoned, gestures they had once made.

The room smelled of powder and pads, and the unkind reek of setting lotion. The hairdresser had been that morning to see to the hair of the women. His visit was less to do with appearance than appearances. The old men hid in the smoking room when the hairdresser came, in order to set up their own evil pong.

It was while the perms and sets and demiwaves were taking shape on a Thursday that Mary was able to join Mr Charteris in the pantry.

He had won her with his golden tongue.

'You're new,' he said. 'I always show the new maids the ropes.'

She knew better than to correct his words. A number of them, being old, spoke like old people couldn't help but do. She'd a lot of time for old people. She'd worked in several homes before, though none as exclusive – meaning expensive – as this. Some of them paid their own bills, others got paid for by children, not without a grumble at the end of the month.

Mr Charteris had arrangements, and that was all Mary had heard, though she had heard one old trout call him a 'scholarship boy' and then whinny with the pleasure being unpleasant gives to those who do not fight it.

Mr Charteris continued: 'Any difficulties at all with the other girls, come straight to me. Don't waste your time going to Mrs How's Yer Father or troubling old Oojama-flip.' He twisted the stud under his bow tie and then levelled off its ends. 'There's nothing I can't tell you about the house. Nothing at all. Man and boy I've been here, starting in the carpenter's yard on crackbacked chairs and coming right through till I got where I am now.'

Mary was unsure what a person might want to know about a house, and where exactly Mr Charteris had got to.

'God, it must be old if *you've* been here all along,' she said, and was delighted when he laughed. He had assertive teeth, every one his own.

'I followed on after only five others like myself. That's not many butlers over the two-seventy-odd years. Not that the earlier ones could rightly be called butlers.'

Mary, who understood from the television that butlers were men who stood still, sneered, and talked posh, asked, 'The work can't have been hard, though?'

Mr Charteris considered the mornings of his life when he, at much the age of this girl, had collaborated in the daily launch of the house, cleaned, polished, dazzling, rebegun, all on the sweat of eight men and sixteen girls, repeating with their bodies actions of the most tedious and exhausting kind in order to give a context to the ease of others, like men blowing bottles from the burning roots of their lungs just to hold scent that would waft off an earlobe unnoticed in the breeze.

'I've had a woman in every room of the house,' said Mr Charteris to Mary.

He revisited the house in the way he preferred in his mind, through the oxters and ribbons and stays and mouthings of the Roses, Daisys, Rubys, Violets, Marias and Elizas who had been drawn by him into each room's mystery, so that he understood the attic through Hetty's red hair and startling milky snores, the music room through the stifled tears and later laughter of Lavender as he lowered the music stool slowly beneath her by swivelling the mahogany discs at either side within her skirts, the ballroom by the chilly biting of Daphne as they pushed together inside the curtains, the kitchen through the blissful humming of Euphemia's skin under his mouth, and later through the regrettable harrying of his own late wife.

'Every room?' said Mary, not interested, nor paying attention, really, not having listened, as people often do not to the old. She just couldn't help, being a trained geriatric nurse, running with the feeble thread. When she found it attached to a cunning rope she was caught by her own decency, the first snare.

Knowing well the sunshine it is to be needed, even by someone who means little, and sensing his distinct, perhaps unrepeatable, advantage, Mr Charteris said to Mary, relying on her tenderness and on his own undimmed brown eyes, 'Every room, my dear, except the pantry.'

These afternoons, the little treats of food given privately, the counterfeit tasks undertaken by Mr Charteris in the aftermath of his making good that late omission, went on beyond the one time it would in principle have taken. Who could say whether Mary had not learned from the old man, just before he sank, the radiant satisfaction of domestic habit, that it was not she who escaped from regulation and certainty into the life of the back of the house, into invented duties and words that were as plain and mysterious as the low windows giving out on to the deeps of the park where no one went any more, or not so that it was known?

The back stairs of the house were cool even in this heat. The service lift creaked on its cables down past the stone stairs to Francis, where he stood with the laundry hamper poised on its mobile ramp, ready to load. He pushed the creaking thing in to the lift, and pulled on the cables, calling upwards, 'All yours, Mary.'

He heard her tug and brake on the cables, and ran up the stone stairs to her, ready to pull out the hamper and help her roll it to the laundry room on the pallet on casters that stood ready in the top corridor. The floors were timber, not lino, up here.

'Come and help me sort it if you can spare the time,' said Mary. 'It's beautiful work.' He supposed at first that she spoke that way on account of having a vocation, as he supposed a nurse must.

But the work *was* beautiful today in the laundry room, its high brief windows letting light in from both sides of the roof, the shelves and wooden floor smelling of dry lavender and lavender wax. Mary and Francis pulled out sleeve after heavy sleeve of laundered white sheet.

'We could do the laundry here if it was brought up to date. There's the room, but no machines. They'd cost. But Lord knows what you cost.'

'It's not rightly me. I drive the van. They wash the sheets.'

'You know what I mean.'

'You look well today, Mary,' said Francis, certain he would not be misunderstood. 'You always look well. It must be encouraging for the residents.'

'Thanks,' said Mary. 'All I am is alive.'

Outside two pigeons skirmished in a lead gutter, the green and pink off their breasts firing through the old glass, their exalted cooing boastful.

'I've a grandmother living at home with me and my friend at the moment. She works with papers. Lately there have been complaints that she's losing her grip. I don't think she is. I think she's being tactful.'

'Tactful?' Mary pushed a pile of sheets to the back of a shelf. It moved with a toppling weight over the papered shelf and then settled against the white wall. 'Who to?'

'In case my friend and I want a bit of space.'

'Do you now?'

'Well, we wouldn't mind *space*. She covers everything with bits of paper. And she brings home worshippers of whatever denomination has irritated her recently.'

'Irritated her?'

'By keeping a messy churchyard. Or, if she can get in, an untidy church. They tend to be rural. She reaches those by bus.'

'She brings them home?'

'Yes, you know. After she's tidied up the place of worship, she attends a service or two and then lures them home. They sit and talk. She draws them out. They frequently return. We've made a number of friends.'

'So she is active and sociable?'

Francis did not like the sound of those words. They described human traits with a functional tongue.

'I love her. When I say we could do with a bit more space, that's all I mean. She takes up a certain amount of room. I want her with us, unless she wants to be away herself. How do I find out what she wants? I don't believe her work *is* slipping. I don't see it. I've only my mother's word for it. Chuck me those draw sheets and I'll go up the steps.'

'You want to know what she wants?'

'I want to know what she wants.'

'Bring her here to look. It's one of the best. The place is beautiful. She could fill her whole room – they get a room to themselves, you know – with pieces of paper. She could have visitors. At least between certain hours. Not in the evening. They get a bath when they want, as long as it's twice a week and they don't use bath oil. That ups the fractures and *that* looks bad. They don't have shepherd's pie every single day. Sister doesn't always open

their letters. The toilets have emergency bells that get
an annual service. There's a weekly hairdresser. There
are socials.'

'It sounds great,' said Francis, his heart flat.

'Yes,' said Mary, 'and it's not free either.'

Francis's grandmother replaced the telephone. She
enjoyed the fact that her daughter Kay did not
recognise her when she called up in the voice of a
learned and exasperated historian or an angry man of
letters who had made allowances for an old woman
long enough.

Indexing had at last lost its charm for Lavender
Maclehose. She had it in mind to get away, and to use
the part of her savings she had not earmarked for these
two dear good boys. There was the funeral account
tidied up, with the undertaker at last convinced about
her plan of having confetti and mimosa – whatever the
time of year – and making sure that six dozen pink roses
were left behind in the vestry for the cleaner.

'I'm home,' called her grandson. 'Do you fancy a cig
while I cut a lettuce?'

'Delicious,' said his grandmother, hoping it would do
for whatever he had said. So much of her time now was
spent day-dreaming. She had it planned. It would be
soon. Her knowledge of rural buses would help.

It was still light in the small garden. Francis cut a pale
crinkled lettuce. It left a woody boss, weeping milk. He
lit his grandmother's cigarette and looked at the gardens
beyond, the wigwams of runner beans with their red
flowers, the tipsy roses and tired children refusing to
leave their darkening climbing frames.

'Don't ever think you must leave unless it's what you
want,' he said to his grandmother. 'We've all the room in

the world here for you, you know that. Pretend I haven't said this.'

Pat had brought the perfect dinner for the three of them off the last shift. They sat in the silvery narrow garden. There was cold soup made out of herbs and cream, a cheese the size of a flat iron, and two slices of a kind of berry cake. They burned a khaki candle to keep off the gnats. It was an old citronella candle from the ironmongery where Francis had once worked. They had enough nails for life.

Lavender had taken care not to tidy up in any depth before she ran away. She said goodnight to Pat and to Francis in her usual brusque fashion, even remembering to cross the bedroom floor again and again as she did most nights.

When she was sure they were asleep, she took her grip and left the two letters on the kitchen counter, beside the kettle. One for her daughter, one for the two men.

She closed the door with a dog-owner's stealth.

The street was drenched with dew and lamplight as she walked down it and out towards the bypass.

It was too early for milkfloats, too late for country buses. She walked more quickly than she had for years. With no one to watch her, she was again young as she made her way to the road that led to the house she had known before Kay was born, the house where she had worked so hard she vowed to work with her brain only, ever after, so that she had worked nights to become a housekeeper of books, a spring-cleaner of the alphabet.

She was on her way back to the house that she had come to miss as you miss the use of your young body, the house she was ready to reinhabit at the end. She dreamed as she made her way along the awakening road of working again at the dusting and ceaseless polishing of wood, the testing of the fine furniture to see it was all in working order so that others might use it, others who did not know that on the piano stool where sat little Miss Veronica there had only that morning been a spin and a flurry at the heart of a whirl of petticoats scented with nothing more rare than lavender wax.

A Story for Europe
Will Self

'*Wir-wir,*' gurgled Humpy, pushing his little fingers into
the bowl of spaghetti Miriam had just cooked for him.
He lifted his hands up to his face and stared hard at the
colloidal web of pasta and cheese. '*Wir müssen expandie-
ren!*' he pronounced solemnly.

'Yes, darling, they *are* like worms, aren't they,' said the
toddler's mother.

Humpy pursed his little lips and looked at her with his
discomfiting bright blue eyes. Miriam held the gaze for a
moment, willing herself to suffuse her own eyes with
tenderness and affection. Blobs of melted cheese fell from
Humpy's hands, but he seemed unconcerned. '*Masse!*' he
crowed after some seconds.

'*Very* messy,' Miriam replied, hating the testiness
that infected her tone. She began dabbing at the
plastic tray of his high chair, smearing the blobs of
cheese and coiling the strayed strands of spaghetti into
edible casts.

Humpy continued staring at the toy he'd made out of
his tea.

'*Masse,*' he said again.

'Put it down, Humpy. Put it in the dish – *in the dish!*'
Miriam felt the clutch on her control slipping.

Humpy's eyes widened still more – a typical prelude
to tears. But he didn't cry, he threw the whole mess on
the just-cleaned floor, and as he did so shouted,
'*Massenfertigung!*' or some such gibberish.

Miriam burst into tears. Humpy calmly licked his fingers and appeared obscurely satisfied.

When Daniel got back from work an hour later, mother and son were still not reconciled. Humpy had struggled and fought and bitten his way through the rituals of pre-bedtime. Every item of clothing that needed to be removed had had to be pulled off his resisting form; he made Miriam drag him protesting every inch of the ascent to the bathroom; and once in the bath he splashed and kicked so much that her blouse and bra were soaked through. Bathtime ended with both of them naked and steaming.

But Daniel saw none of this. He saw only his blue-eyed handsome boy, with his angelic brown curls framing his adorable, chubby face. He put his bag down by the hall table and gathered Humpy up in his arms. 'Have you been a good boy while Daddy was at the office – '

'You don't have an office!' snapped Miriam, who like Humpy was in Teri-towelling, but assumed in her case for reasons of necessity rather than comfort.

'Darling, darling . . . what's the matter?' Carrying the giggling Humpy, whose hands were entwined in his hair, Daniel advanced towards his wife.

'*Darlehen, hartes Darlehen,*' gurgled Humpy, seemingly mimicking his father.

'If you knew what a merry dance he's led me today, you wouldn't be *quite* so affectionate to the little bugger.' Miriam shrank away from Daniel's kiss. She was worried that, if she softened, let down her Humpy-guard at all, she might start to cry again.

Daniel sighed. 'It's just his age. *All* children go through a difficult phase at around two and a half; Humpy's no exception – '

'That may be so. But not all children are so aggressive. Honestly, Daniel, I swear you don't get to see the half of it. It's not as if I don't give him every ounce of love that I have to give; and he flings it back in my face, along with a lot of gibberish!' And with this Miriam did begin to cry, racking sobs which wrenched her narrow shoulders.

Daniel pulled Miriam to him and stroked her hair. Even Humpy seemed distressed by this turn of events. '*Mutter*,' he said wonderingly, '*Mutter*,' and squirmed around in his father's arms, so as to share in the family embrace.

'See,' said Daniel, 'of course he loves his mother. Now you open a bottle of that nice Chablis, and I'll put young Master Humpy down for the night.'

Miriam blinked back her tears. 'I suppose you're right. You take him up then.' She bestowed a glancing kiss on the top of Humpy's head. Father and son disappeared up the stairs. The last thing Miriam heard before they rounded the half-landing was more of Humpy's peculiar baby talk. '*Mutter – Mutter – Muttergesellschaft*' was what it sounded like. Miriam tried hard to hear this as some expression of love towards herself. Tried hard – but couldn't manage it.

Daniel laid Humpy down in his cot. 'Who's a very sleepy boy then?' he asked.

Humpy looked up at him; his blue eyes were still bright, untainted with fatigue. '*Wende!*' said Humpy cheerily. '*Wende-Wende-Wende!*' He drew his knees up to his chest and kicked them out.

'Ye-es, that's right.' Daniel pulled the clutch of covers up over the bunched little boy. 'Wendy *will* be here to look after you in the morning, because it's Mummy's day to go to work, isn't it?' He leant down to kiss his son, marvelling – as ever – at the tight, intense feeling the flesh of his flesh provoked in him. 'Goodnight, little love.' He turned on the nightlight with its slow-moving carousel of leaping bunnies and clicked off the main light. As Daniel went back downstairs he could still hear Humpy gurgling to himself, '*Wende-Wende*,' contentedly.

But there was little content to be had at the Greens' oval scrubbed-pine kitchen table that evening. Miriam Green had stopped crying, but an atmosphere of fraught weepiness prevailed. 'Perhaps I'm too bloody old for this,' she said to Daniel, thumping a steaming casserole down so that flecks of onion, flageolets and juice spilled on to the table.' I nearly hit him today, Daniel, hit him!'

'You musn't be so hard on yourself, Miriam. He is a handful – and you know that it's always the mother who gets the worst of it. Listen, as soon as this job is over I'll take some more time off – '

'Daniel, it isn't that that's the problem.'

And it wasn't, for Miriam Green couldn't complain about Daniel. He did far more childcare than most fathers, and certainly more than any father who was trying to get a landscape-gardening business going in the teeth of a recession. Nor was Miriam cut off from the world of work by her motherhood, the way so many women were, isolated then demeaned by their loss of status. She had insisted on continuing with her career as a journalist after Humphrey was born, although she had accepted a jobshare in order to spend two and a half days a week at home. Wendy, the part-time nanny who covered for Miriam during the rest of the week, was, quite simply, a treasure. Intelligent, efficient and as devoted to Humpy as he was to her.

No, when Miriam Green let fly the remark about being 'too old', her husband knew what it was that was really troubling her. It was the same thing that had troubled her throughout her pregnancy. The first trimester may have been freighted with nausea, the second characterised by a kind of skittish sexiness, and the third swelling to something resembling bulgy beatitude, but throughout it all Miriam Green had felt deeply uneasy. She had emphatically declined the amniocentesis offered by her doctor, although at forty-one the hexagonal chips were not quite stacked in her favour.

'I don't believe in tinkering with destiny,' she had told Daniel, who, although he had not said so, thought the more likely reason was that Miriam felt she had tinkered with destiny too much already, and that this would, in a mysterious way, be weighed in the balance against her. Daniel was sensitive to her feelings, and although they talked around the subject, neither of them ever came right out with it and voiced the awful fear that the baby Miriam was carrying might turn out to be *not quite right*.

In the event the birth was a pure joy – and a revelation. Miriam and Daniel had lingered at home for the first five hours of the labour, mindful of all the premature hospital-dashes their friends had made. When they eventually got to the hospital Miriam's cervix was eight centimetres dilated. It was too late for an epidural, or even pethidine. Humphrey was born exactly fifty-one minutes later, as Miriam squatted, bellowing, on what looked to Daniel suspiciously like a school gym mat.

One moment he was watching the sweating, distending bulk of his wife, her face pushed about by pain; the next he was holding a blue-red ball of howling new vitality. Humphrey was perfect in every way. He scored ten out of ten on the first assessment. His features were no more oriental than those of any other new-born Caucasian baby. Daniel held him tight, and uttered muttered prayers to the idea of a god that might have arranged things so perfectly.

The comfortable Victorian house in Muswell Hill the Greens called home had long since been tricked out with enough baby equipment to cope with sextuplets. The room designated as the young master's baby had had a mural of a rainforest painted on its walls by an artist friend, complete with myriad examples of biodiversity. The cot was from Heal's, the buggy by Silver Cross. There were no less than three back-up Milton sterilisers.

Daniel had worried that Miriam was becoming obsessive in the weeks preceding the birth, and after they brought Humpy home from the hospital he watched her closely for any signs of creeping depression, but none came. Humphrey thrived, putting on weight like a diminutive boxer preparing for life's title fight. Sometimes Daniel and Miriam worried that they doted on him too much, but mostly they both felt glad that they had waited to become parents, and that their experience and maturity was part of the reason their child seemed so pacific. He hardly ever cried, or was colicky. He even cut his first two teeth without any fuss. He was, Daniel pronounced, tossing Humpy up in the air while they all giggled, 'a mensch'.

Daniel and Miriam delighted in each stage of Humpy's development. Daniel took roll after roll of out-of-focus shots of his blue-eyed boy, and Miriam pasted them into scrapbooks, then drew elaborate decorative borders around them. Humpy's first backwards crawl, frontwards crawl, trembling step, unassisted bowel movement, all had their memento. But then, at around two, their son's smooth and steady path of development appeared to waver.

Humpy's giggles and gurgles had always been expressive. He was an infant ready to smile, and readier still to give voice. But at that time, when from many many readings of the relevant literature his parents knew he should be beginning to form recognisable words, starting to iterate correctly, Humpy changed. He still gave voice, but the 'Da-das' and 'Ma-mas' garbled in his little mouth; and were then augmented with more guttural gibberish.

Their friends didn't really seem to notice. As far as they were concerned it was just a toddler's rambunctious burbling, but both Daniel and Miriam grew worried. Miriam took Humpy to the family doctor, and then at her instigation to a specialist. Was there some hidden cleft in Humpy's palate? No, said the specialist, who examined Humpy thoroughly and soothingly. Everything was all right inside Humpy's mouth and larynx. Mrs Green really shouldn't be too anxious. Children develop in many diverse ways; if anything – and this wasn't the specialist's particular expertise, he was not a child psychologist – Humpy's scrambled take on the business of language acquisition was probably a sign of an exceptional burgeoning intellect.

Still, relations between mother and son did deteriorate. Miriam told Daniel that she felt Humpy was becoming strange to her. She found his tantrums increasingly hard to deal with. She asked Daniel again and again, 'Is it me? Is it that I'm not relating to him properly?' And again and again Daniel reassured her that it was 'just a stage'.

Sometimes, pushing Humpy around the Quadrant, on her way to the shops on Fortis Green Road, Miriam would pause and look out over the suburban sprawl of North London. In her alienation from her own child, the city of her birth was, she felt, becoming a foreign land.

The barely buried anxieties about her age, and how this might be a factor in what was happening to Humpy, clawed their way through the sub-soil of her psyche.

Herr Doktor Martin Zweijärig, Deputy Director of the Venture Capital Research Department of Deutsche Bank, stood at the window of his office on the twentieth storey of the Bank's headquarters building looking out over the jumbled horizon of Frankfurt. All about him, the other concrete peaks of 'Mainhattan', the business and banking district, rose up to the lowering sky. Zweijärig's office window flowed around a corner of the Bank's building, and this, together with his elevated perspective, afforded him a view of the city cut up into vertical slices by the surrounding office blocks.

To his left, he could view an oblong of the university, and beyond it the suburb of Bockenheim; to his right the gleaming steel trapezoid of the Citibank building bisected the roof of the main station, and beyond it the old district of Sachsenhausen. Zweijärig couldn't see the River Main – but he knew it was there. And straight in front of him the massive eminence of the Messeturm, the highest office building in Europe, blotted-out most of the town centre, including, thankfully, the mangled Modernism of the Zweil shopping centre. Zweijärig had once, idly, calculated that, if a straight line were projected from his office window, down past the right-hand flank of the Messeturm at the level of the fifteenth storey, it should meet the earth two thousand and fifty-seven metres further on, right in the middle of the Goethehaus on Hirschgrab Strasse; forming a twanging, invisible chord, connecting past and present, and perhaps future.

'We must expand!' The phrase with its crude message of commercial triumphalism kept running through Zweijärig's mind, exhorting his inner ear. Why did Kleist feel the need to state the obvious in quite so noisy a fashion? And so early in the morning? Zweijärig didn't resent Kleist's elevation above him in the hierarchy of the Venture Capital Division – it made sense. He was, after all, at fifty-five six years Zweijärig's junior; and even though they had both been with the Bank the same number of years, it was Kleist who had the urge, the drive, to push for expansion, to grapple with the elephantine bureaucracy the Treuhand had become and seek out new businesses in the East for the Bank to take an interest in.

But the rescheduling of the directors' meeting for 7.30 a.m., and the trotting-out of such tawdry pabulums! Why, this morning Kleist had even had the temerity to talk of mass marketing as the logical goal of the Division. 'The provision of seed capital, hard loans even, for what – on the surface – may appear to be ossified, redundant concerns, can be approached at a mass level. We need to get the information concerning the services we offer to the widest possible sector of the business community. If this entails a kind of mass marketing then so be it.'

Zweijärig sighed deeply. A dapper man, of medium height, with a dark, sensual face, he was as ever dressed in a formal, sober, three-piece suit. This was one Frau Doktor Zweijärig had bought at the English shop, Barries, on Goethestrasse. Zweijärig liked the cut of English business suits, and also their conservatism. Perhaps it was because he wasn't a native Frankurter, but rather a displaced Sudetenlander, that Zweijärig felt the brashness of his adoptive city so keenly. He sighed again, and pushed his spectacles up on his forehead, so

that steel rims became enmeshed in wire-wool hair.
With thumb and forefinger he massaged his eyes.

He felt airy today, insubstantial. Normally the detail of
his work was so readily graspable that it provided his mind
with more than enough traction, adhesion to the world.
But for the past few days he had felt his will skittering about
like a puck on an ice rink. He couldn't seem to hold on to
any given thought for more than a few seconds.

Maybe it was a bug of some kind? His daughter,
Astrid, had called the previous evening from Stuttgart
and said that she definitely had a viral infection. She'd
stayed with them at the weekend – perhaps that was it?
Zweijärig couldn't remember feeling quite so unenthu-
siastic about work on a Tuesday morning. Or was it that
Kleist's appointment had irked him more than he
realised. Right now he would have rather been in the
Kleinmarkthalle, buying sausage or pig's ears from
Schreiber's; or else at home with Gertrud, pruning the
roses on the lower terrace. He conjured up a vision of
their house, its wooden walls and wide glass windows
merging with the surrounding woodland. It was only
twenty kilometres outside Frankfurt, on the north bank
of the river, but a world away.

Zweijärig fondled the heavy fob of his car keys in the
pocket of his trousers. He pushed the little nipple that
opened the central locking on the Mercedes, imagining
the car springing into life, rear lights flashing. He
pictured it, under autopilot, backing, filling, then driving up from the underground car-park to sit by the kerb
in front of the building, waiting to take him home.

'Childish,' he muttered aloud, 'bloody childish.'

'Herr Doktor?' said Frau Schelling, Zweijärig's secre-
tary, who he hadn't realised had entered the room. 'Did
you say something?'

'Nothing – it's nothing, Frau Schelling.' He summoned himself, turned from the window to confront her. 'Are those the files on Unterweig?'

'Yes, Herr Doktor. Would you like to go over them with me now?' Zweijärig thought he detected a note of exaggerated concern in her voice, caught up in the bucolic folds of her Swabian accent.

'No, no, that's all right. As long as the details of the parent company are there as well – '

'Herr Doktor, I'm sorry to interrupt, but Unterweig has no parent company, if you recall. It was only properly incorporated in May of last year.'

'Incorporated? Oh yes, of course, how foolish of me. Please, Frau Schelling, I'm feeling a little faint. You wouldn't mind terribly getting me a glass of water from the cooler?'

'Of course not, Herr Doktor, of course not.'

She put the folder down on the desk and hustled out of the room. Really, thought Zweijärig, I must pull myself together – such weakness in front of Frau Schelling. He pulled out the heavy leather chair, the one he had inhabited for the past sixteen years, brought with him from the posting in Munich. He allowed the smell and feel of the thing to absorb him. He picked up the folders and tamped them into a neat oblong, then laid them down again, opened the cover of the first and began to read:

Unterweig is a metal-working shop specialising in the manufacture of basic steel structures for children's playground equipment. The main plant is situated on the outskirts of Potsdam, and there is an office complex in the north-central district. As ever in these cases it is difficult to reach an effective

calculation of capitalisation or turnover. Since May
1992, the shop has managed to achieve incorpora-
tion despite a 78 per cent fall in orders . . .

The words swam in front of Zweijärig's eyes. Why
bother, he thought. I've read so many reports like this,
considered so many investment opportunities, what can
this one possibly have to offer that any of the others
didn't? And why is it that we persist in this way with the
Easterners? He grimaced, remembering that he himself
had once been like the Easterners – no, not like them,
worse off than them. There had been no one-to-one
conversion rate for the little that the Russians had
allowed him to take.

A thirteen-year-old boy carrying a canvas bag with
some bread in it, a pair of socks and two books. One, the
poems of Hölderlin, the other a textbook on calculus,
with most of the pages loose in the binding. He could
barely remember the long walk into exile any more. It
seemed to belong to someone else's past, it was too lurid,
too nasty, too brutal, too sad for the man he'd become.
Flies gathering on a dead woman's tongue.

Had the fields really been that beautiful in Bohemia? He
seemed to remember them that way. Smaller fields than
those in the West, softer, and fringed by cherry trees always
in bloom. It can't have been so. The cherry trees could only
have blossomed for a couple of weeks each year, and yet
that's what had stayed with him: the clutches of petals
pushed and then burst by the wind, creating a warm,
fragrant snowfall. He couldn't face meeting with Bocklin
and Schiele at the Frankfurter Hof. He'd rather have a few
glasses of stuff somewhere, loosen this damn tie . . .
Zweijärig's hand went to his neck without him noticing,
and shaking fingers tugged at the knot.

On her way back from the water-cooler Frau Schelling saw her boss's face half-framed by one of the glass
panels siding his office. He looked, she thought, old, very
old for a man of sixty-one. And in the past few days he
seemed unable to concentrate on anything much. Herr
Doktor Zweijärig, who was always the very epitome of
correctness, of efficiency. She wondered whether he
might have suffered a minor stroke. She had heard of
such things happening – and the person concerned not
even noticing, not even *being able* to notice; the part of
the brain that should be doing such noticing suffused
with blood. It would be uncomfortable for Frau Schelling to call Frau Doktor Zweijärig and voice her anxieties
– but worse if she did nothing. She entered the office
quietly and placed the glass of water by his elbow, then
silently footed out.

Miriam placed the feeding cup by Humpy's cot and
paused for a moment looking down at him. It was such a
cliché to say that children looked angelic when they
slept, and in Humpy's case it was metaphoric under-
statement. Humpy appeared angelic when awake; asleep
he was like a cherry blossom lodged in the empyrean, a
fragment of the divinity. Miriam sighed heavily and
clawed a hank of her dark corkscrew curls back from
her brow. She'd brought the feeding cup full of apple
juice in to forestall Humpy calling for her immediately
on awaking. He could get out of his cot easily enough by
himself, but she knew he wouldn't until he'd finished the
juice.

    Miriam silently footed out of Humpy's room. She just
needed five more minutes to herself, to summon herself.
It had been an agonised night on Humpy's account. Not
that he'd kept Miriam and Daniel up personally – he

never did that – but it had been a night of reckoning, of debating and of finally deciding that they should keep the appointment with the child psychologist that Dr Peppard had made for them for the following day.

Daniel had gone off to work just after dawn, giving the half-asleep Miriam a snuffly kiss on the back of her neck. 'I'll meet you at the clinic,' he said.

'You be there,' Miriam grunted in reply.

Dr Peppard had shared their misgivings about consulting the child psychologist, their worries that, even at two and a half, Humpy might apprehend the institutional atmosphere of the clinic and feel stigmatised, pathologised, mysteriously different to other toddlers. But more than that, she worried that the Greens were losing their grip on reality; she had seldom seen a happier, better-adjusted child than Humpy. Dr Peppard had great confidence in Philip Weston – he was as good at divining adult malaises as he was those of children. If anyone could help the Greens to deal with their overweening affection for their child – which Dr Peppard thought privately was the beginning of an extreme, hot-housing tendency – then it would be Philip Weston.

Miriam now lay, face crushed into pillow, one ear registering the *Today Programme* – John Humphreys withering at some junior commissioner in Brussels – the other cocked for Humpy's awakening, his juice-slurping, his agglutinative wake-Miriam-up call.

This came soon enough. '*Bemess-bemess-bemess – !*' he cried, shaking the side of his cot so that it squeaked and creaked. '*Bemessungsgrundlage,*' he garbled.

'All right, Humpy,' Miriam called out to him. 'All right, Humpy love, I'm coming!' then buried her head still further in the pillow. But she couldn't shut it out:

'*Bemess-bemess-bemessungsgrundlage!*' Better to get up and deal with him.

An hour or so later Miriam was sitting at her dressing table, which was set in the bay window of the master bedroom, with Humpy on her lap. It was a beautiful morning in late spring and the Greens' garden – which Daniel lavished all of his professional skills on – was an artfully disordered riot of verdancy. Miriam sighed, pulling the squirming Humpy to her breast. Life could be so sweet, so good; perhaps Dr Peppard was right and she was needlessly anxious about Humpy. 'I *do* love you so much, Humpy – you're my favourite boy.' She kissed the soft bunch of curls atop his sweet head.

Humpy struggled in her embrace and reached out to one of the bottles on the dressing table. Miriam picked it up and pressed it into his fat little palm. 'This is kohl, Humpy – can you say that, "kohl"? Try to.'

Humpy looked at the vial of make-up intently; his small frame felt tense in Miriam's arms. '*Kohl,*' he said. '*Kohl!*' he reiterated with more emphasis.

Miriam broke into peals of laughter. 'That's a clever Humpy!' She stood up, feeling the curious coiled heft of the child as she pulled him up with her. She waltzed Humpy a few steps around the room.

'*Kohl!*' he cried out merrily, and mother and son giggled and whirled; and would have gone on giggling and whirling were it not for the sound of the front door bell.

'Bugger!' said Miriam, stopping the dance. 'That'll be the postman, we'd better go and see what he wants.'

The change in Humpy was instantaneous – almost frighteningly so. '*Pohl!*' he squealed. '*Pohl-Pohl-Pohl!*' and then all his limbs flew out, his foot catching Miriam in her lower abdomen.

She nearly dropped him. The moment before, the moment of apparently mutual comprehension was gone, and in its place was a grizzling gulf. 'Oh Humpy – please, Humpy!' Miriam struggled to control his flailing arms. 'It's OK, it's OK,' she soothed him, but really it was she who needed the soothing.

Philip Weston entered the waiting room of the Gruton Child Guidance Clinic moving silently on the balls of his feet. He was a large, adipose man, who wore baggy corduroy trousers to disguise his thick legs and bulky arse. Like many very big men he had an air of stillness and poise about him. His moon face was cratered with jolly dimples, and his bright-orange hair stood up in a cartoon flammable ruff. He was an extremely competent clinician, with an ability to build a rapport with even the most disturbed children.

The scene that met his forensically attuned eyes was pacific. The Green family were relaxed in the bright sunny waiting room. Miriam sat leafing through a magazine, Daniel sat by her, working away at the occupational dirt beneath his nails, using the marline-spike on his clasp knife. At their feet was Humpy. Humpy had, with Daniel's assistance, in the fifteen minutes since they'd arrived at the clinic, managed to build a fairly extensive network of Brio toy-train tracks, incorporating a swing bridge and a level crossing. Of his own accord he had also connected up a train, some fifteen cars long, and this he was pushing along with great finesse, making the appropriate 'Woo-woo' noises.

'I'm Philip Weston,' said the child psychologist. 'You must be Miriam and Daniel, and this is – ?'

'Humpy – I mean Humphrey.' Miriam Green lurched to her feet, edgy at once.

'Please.' Philip damped her down, and knelt down himself by the little boy. 'Hello, Humpy, how are you today?'

Humpy left off mass-transportation activities and looked quizzically at the clownish man, his sharp blue eyes meeting Philip's waterier gaze. '*Besser*,' he said at length.

'Better?' queried Philip, mystified.

'*Besser*,' Humpy said again, with solemn emphasis. '*Besserwessi!*' and as if this gobbledygook settled the matter, he turned back to the Brio.

Philip Weston regained the foundation of his big legs. 'Shall we go in,' he said to the Greens, and indicated the open door of his consulting room.

Neither Miriam nor Daniel had had any idea of what to expect from this encounter, but in the event they were utterly charmed by Philip Weston. His consulting room was more in the manner of a bright, jolly nursery, a logical extension of the waiting room outside. While Humpy toddled about, picking up toys from plastic crates, or pulling down picture books from the shelves, the child psychologist chatted with his parents. So engaging and informal was his manner that neither Miriam nor Daniel felt they were being interviewed or assessed in any way – although that was, in fact, what was happening.

Philip Weston chatted their worries out of them. His manner was so relaxed, his demeanour so unjudgmental, that they both felt able to voice their most chilling fears. Was Humpy perhaps autistic? Or brain-damaged? Was Miriam's age in some way responsible for his learning difficulty? To all of these Philip Weston was able to provide instant and total refutation. 'You can certainly set yourselves at rest as far as any autism is concerned,' he

told them. 'Humpy engages emotionally and sympathe-
tically with the external world; as you can see now, he's
using that stuffed toy to effect a personation. No autistic
child ever engages in such role-playing activity.'

Nor, according to Philip, was Humpy in any way
retarded: 'He's using two or more coloured pencils in
that drawing, and he's already forming recognisable
shapes. I think I can tell you with some authority that,
if anything, this represents advanced, rather than retarded, ability for a child of his age. If there is a real
problem here, Mr and Mrs Green, I suspect it may be to
do with a gift rather than a deficiency.'

After twenty minutes or so of chatting and quietly
observing Humpy, who continued to make use of Philip
Weston's superb collection of toys and diversions, the
child psychologist turned his attention directly to him.
He picked up a small tray full of outsized marbles from
his desk and called to the toddler, 'Humpy, come and
look at these.' Humpy came jogging across the room,
smiling broadly. In his cute, Osh-Kosh bib 'n' braces, his
brown curls framing his chubby face, he looked a picture
of health and radiance.

Philip Weston selected one of the marbles and gave it to
Humpy. 'Now, Humpy,' he said, 'if I give you two of
these marbles' – he rattled the tray – 'will you give me that
marble back?' Without even needing to give this exchange
any thought Humpy thrust the first marble in the child
psychologist's face. Philip took it, put it in the tray, selected
two other shiny marbles and gave them to him. Humpy
grinned broadly. Philip turned to Miriam and Daniel
saying, 'This is really quite exceptional comprehension
for a child Humpy's age – ' He turned back to Humpy.

'Now, Humpy, if I give you two of these remaining
marbles, will you give me those two marbles back?'

Humpy stared at Philip for some seconds, while storm clouds gathered in his blue, blue eyes. The little boy's brow furrowed, and his fist closed tightly around his two marbles. '*Besserwessi!*' he spat at Philip, and then, '*Grundgesetz!*'.

It was to Philip's credit, and a fantastic exemplar of his clinical skills, that he didn't react at all adversely to these bits of high-pitched nonsense, but merely put the question again: 'These two marbles, Humpy, for your two, what do you say?'

Humpy opened his hand and looked at the two blue marbles he had in his possession. Philip selected two equally shiny blue marbles from the tray and proffered them. There was silence for some moments while the two parties eyed one another's merchandise. Then Humpy summoned himself. He put one marble very carefully in the side pocket of his overalls, and the other in the bib pocket. This accomplished, he said to Philip with great seriousness, '*Finanzausgleichgesetz,*' turned neatly on his heels, and went back to the scribbling he'd been doing before the child psychologist called him over.

Daniel Green sighed heavily, and passed a hand through his hair. 'Well, now you've seen it, Philip – that's the Humpy we deal with most of the time. He talks this . . . this . . . I know I shouldn't say it, but it's gibberish, isn't it?'

'Hmmm . . .' Philip was clearly giving the matter some thought before replying. 'We-ell, I agree, it doesn't sound like anything recognisably meaningful, but there is definitely something going on here, Humpy is communicating *something*, something that he thinks we might comprehend. There's great deliberation in what he's saying . . . I don't know, I don't know . . .' He shook his head.

'What?' Miriam was sitting forward on the edge of her
chair; she was trying to remain calm, but her troubled
expression betrayed her. 'What do you think? Please,
don't hold anything back from us.'

'It could be pure speculation. It's something I've never
seen before. I tell you, if I didn't know any better I'd be
prepared to hazard the idea that young Humpy was
originating some kind of idiolect, you know, a private
language. His cognitive skills are, as I said, quite
remarkably developed for his age. If you don't mind,
I'd like to get a second opinion here.'

'What would that entail?' asked Miriam. She was
clearly appalled by this turn of events, but Daniel, by
contrast, was leaning forward, engaged, intrigued.

'Well, it just so happens that we have a Dr Grauerholtz
visiting us here at the Gruton at the moment. This is a
marvellous opportunity. He's a former director of the
clinic, now based at the Bettelheim Institute in Chicago,
and he's without doubt the foremost expert on human-
language acquisition in either Europe or the USA. If he's
available I'd like him to pop in right away and have a chat
with Humpy as well. See if we can get to the bottom of
this young man's verbal antics. What do you say?'

'What is the basis of assessment?'

'The same as it's always been.'

'Meaning . . .?'

'Meaning that they did have an open order book, that
they did have a capital fund – of some sort. Meaning that
both have been subject to the one-on-one conversion
rate, and those monies remain in escrow. Meaning that
precisely, Herr Doktor.'

'Yes, yes, of course, I know all of that. I know all of
that.'

It was late in the morning and Zweijärig was feeling no better – perhaps worse. He'd groped his way through the Unterweig file and now was attempting to discuss its contents with Hassell, his capitalisation expert. At least he'd taken the leap and got Frau Schelling to cancel the meeting with Bocklin and Schiele. 'The unheard-of must be spoken.'

'I'm sorry, Herr Doktor?' Hassell was looking curiously at his boss. Zweijärig noted, inconsequentially, how pink Hassell's forehead was. Pink fading to white at the hairline, just like a slice of ham.

'Ah, um, well . . .' I spoke aloud? Zweijärig fumbled the ball of thought. What is this – am I really losing my marbles? 'I mean to say, the conversion rate, Hassell, it remains as stupid today as when Kohl proposed it. It's wrecked our chances of building the economy the way we might wish to. It doesn't reflect the constitution – such as it was; and it doesn't accord with the law governing redistribution of fiscal apportionments to the Länder.'

Hassell was staring hard at Zweijärig during this speech. It was about the closest he could remember his boss getting to discussing politics directly in the four years they'd worked together. He normally skated around such topics, avoiding them with something approaching flippancy. Hassell steepled his plump fingers on the edge of the desk, pursed his plump lips, and ventured a query. 'So, Herr Doktor, would you have favoured Pohl's proposal? Do you think things would have gone that much smoother?'

'Pohl-Kohl. Kohl-Pohl. It hardly matters which bloody joker we have sitting on top of the Reichstag. We're a nation of displaced people, Herr Hassell. We're displaced from our past, we're displaced from our land, we're displaced from each other. That's the European ideal for you, eh – we're closer to people in Marseilles or Manchester than we are to those in Magdeburg. It's an ideal of mass society rather than homeland, ach!'

Zweijärig was, Hassell noted, breathing heavily, panting almost. His tie was loosened, the top button of his shirt undone. Hassell didn't wish to be intrusive, but he ought really to enquire. 'Are you feeling all right, Herr Doktor?'

'All right, yes, yes, Herr Hassell, I feel all right. I feel like the smart-aleck Westerner I've become, eh? Wouldn't you say?'

'It's not my position, Herr Doktor – '

'No, no, of course not, of course not. It's not your position. I'm sorry, Herr Hassell, I'm not myself today, I'm like Job on his dungheap – you know that one, d'you? It's in the Stadel, you should go and look at it. *Job on his Dungheap*. Except in *our* case the dungheap is built of glass and steel, hmm?'

'Dungheap, Herr Doktor?' said Hassell, trying to look unobtrusively over his shoulder, trying to see whether Frau Schelling was in the outer office.

'Playing with shit, Herr Hassell, playing with shit. Have you ever heard the expression that money *is* shit, Herr Hassell?'

'Herr Doktor?'

'Money *is* shit. No, well, I suppose not. Y'know, there are ghosts here in Frankfurt, Herr Hassell, you can see them if you squint. You can see them walking about – the ghosts of the past. This city is built on money, so they say. Perhaps it's built on shit too, hmm?'

And with this gnomic – if not crazy – remark, Herr Doktor Martin Zweijärig stood up, passed a sweaty hand across his brow, and made for the door of his office, calling over his shoulder, 'I'm going for a glass of stuff, Herr Hassell. If you would be so good, please tell Frau Schelling I'll be back in a couple of hours.' Then he was gone.

Hassell sighed heavily. The old man was unwell, disturbed even. He was clearly disoriented; perhaps Hassell should stop him leaving the bank building? Ethics and propriety did battle in the arid processes of Hassell's mind for some seconds, until ethics won – narrowly.

Hassell got up and quit the office at a near-jog, the bunches of fat above his broad hips jigging like panniers on a donkey. But when he reached the lifts Zweijärig had gone. He turned back to the office and met Frau Schelling. 'The Deputy Direktor, Frau Schelling, do you think – ?'

'I think he's ill, Herr Hassell – he's behaving very oddly. I called Frau Doktor Zweijärig just now. I hated going behind his back like that, but – '

'You did the right thing, Frau Schelling. What did Frau Doktor Zweijärig say?'

'Oh, she's noticed it as well. She's driving into town right now. She says she'll be here within the hour. But where has he gone?'

'He said something about getting a glass of stuff. Do you think he's gone to Sachsenhausen?'

'I doubt it, he can't stand the GIs there. No, there's a tavern near the station he often goes to. I'll bet he's gone there now.' Frau Schelling shook her head sorrowfully. 'Poor man, I do hope he's all right.'

'Miriam and Daniel Green, this is Dr Grauerholtz . . . and this is Humpy.' Philip Weston stood in the middle of his consulting room making the introductions.

Dr Grauerholtz was a tiny little egg of a man, bald, bifocaled, and wearing a quite electric blue suit. The contrast between the two psychologists was straightforwardly comic, and despite the seriousness of the situation, Daniel and Miriam exchanged surreptitious grins and jointly raised their eyebrows.

'Hello,' said Dr Grauerholtz warmly. He had a thick but not unpleasant German accent. 'Philip tells me that we have a most unusual young fellow with us today – you must be very proud of him.'

'Proud?' Miriam Green was becoming agitated again. Dr Grauerholtz and Philip Weston exchanged meaningful glances. Dr Grauerholtz indicated that they should all sit down. Then, with rapid, jerky movements he stripped off his funny blue jacket, threw it over a chair, reversed the chair, and sat down on it facing them with his elbows crossed on the back.

'I don't think I will be in any way upsetting you, Mr and Mrs Green, if I tell you that my colleague has managed to do a rudimentary Stanford-Binet test on Master Humpy – '

'Stanford-Binet?' Miriam was becoming querulous.

'I'm sorry, so-called intelligence test. Obviously such things are very speculative with such a young child, but we suspect that Humpy's IQ may be well up in the hundred and sixties. He is, we believe, an exceptionally bright young fellow. Now, if you don't mind . . .'

Dr Grauerholtz dropped backwards off the chair on to his knees and then crawled towards Humpy across the expanse of carpet. Humpy, who had payed no attention to Dr Grauerholtz's arrival, was playing with some building blocks in the corner of the room. He had managed to construct a sort of pyramid, or ziggurat, the top of which was level with the first shelf of a bookcase, and now he was running toy cars up the side of this edifice and parking them neatly by the spines of the books.

'That's a good castle you've got there, Humpy,' said Dr Grauerholtz. 'Do you like castles?'

Humpy stopped what he was doing and regarded the semi-recumbent world authority on human-language acquisition with an expression that would have been called contemptuous in an older individual. '*Grundausbildung!*' he piped, scooting one of the toy cars along the shelf. Dr Grauerholtz appeared rather taken aback, and sat back on his heels. Daniel and Miriam gave each other weary looks.

'*Grundausbildung?*' Dr Grauerholtz repeated the gibberish with an interrogative-sounding swoop at the end. Humpy stopped what he was doing, tensed, and turned to give the doctor his full attention. '*Ja,*' he said after a few moments, '*grundausbildung.*'

'*Grundausbildung für . . .?*' gargled the doctor.

'*Für bankkreise,*' Humpy replied, and smiled broadly.

The doctor scratched the few remaining hairs on his head, before saying, 'Humpy, *verstehen sie Deutsch?*'

'*Ja,*' Humpy came back, and giggled. '*Geschäft Deutsch.*' Then he resumed playing with the toy car, as if none of this bizarre exchange were of any account.

Dr Grauerholtz stood up and came back to where the adults were sitting. They were all staring at him with frank astonishment, none more so than Miriam Green. To look at her you might have thought she was in the presence of some prophet, or messiah. 'Doc-Doctor Grau-Grauerholtz,' she stuttered, 'c-can you understand what Humpy is saying?'

'Oh yes,' the Doctor replied. He was now grinning as widely as Humpy. 'Quite well, I think. You see, your

son is speaking . . . How can I put it? He's speaking what
you would call "business German".'

' "Business German"?' queried Philip Weston. 'Isn't
that a bit unusual for an English child of two and a half?'

Dr Grauerholtz had taken his bifocals off and was
cleaning them with a small soft cloth that he'd taken from
his trouser pocket. He looked at the three faces that
gawped at him with watery, myopic eyes, and then said,
'Yes, yes, I suppose a bit unusual, but hardly a handicap.'
He smiled, a small wry smile. 'Some people might say it
was a great asset – especially in today's European
situation, yes?'

Humpy chose that moment to push over the pyramid
of building blocks he'd made. They fell with a delightful
local crash; and Humpy began to laugh. It was the happy,
secure laugh of a well-loved child – if a tad on the
guttural side.

They found Herr Doktor Martin Zweijärig sitting on the
pavement outside the station. His suit was scuffed-about
and dirty, his face was sweaty and contorted. All around
him the human flotsam roiled: Turkish guest workers,
junkies, asylum-seekers and tourists. There was hardly an
ethnic German to be found in this seedy quarter of the
European financial capital. Zweijärig was conscious, but
barely so. The stroke had robbed him of his strength – he
was as weak as a two-year-old child; and quite naturally –
he was talking gibberish.

Maître Mussard's Bequest
Patrick Süskind

Ceaselessly occupied with his curious discoveries,
Mussard worked himself into such a fever over these
thoughts that they would eventually have entangled his
mind in madness, had not death torn him away from
them by a strange and cruel illness: luckily for his
reason, but not for his sorrowing friends to whom he
was dear and valued.

Rousseau, Confessions

These few pages are addressed to some unknown reader
of a later age who has the courage to face the truth and
the strength to bear it. The feeble-spirited may flee my
words like fire, for I have nothing comforting to impart.
I must make haste for I have but a short time left to live.
The mere act of writing a few sentences demands a
super-human exertion, which would be far beyond me,
but for an inner compulsion that drives me to pass on my
knowledge and its implications to the future world.

The doctors say I am suffering from *Paralysis stomacho-
sa*, but the source of this malady is known only to me. It
consists of a rapidly developing paralysis of my limbs and
inner organs. Night and day it compels me to sit bolt
upright in bed, supported by cushions, with a writing
pad on the blanket by my left hand – the right hand
being completely immovable. Turning the pages is the
task of my faithful servant Manet, to whom I have

bequeathed the care of my estate. For three weeks I have taken only liquid nourishment, and for the past two days even swallowing a mouthful of water causes intolerable pain. But I must not dwell any longer on my present condition. I must devote all my remaining strength to describing my discovery. First of all, a few words about myself.

Jean-Jacques Mussard. I was born in Genf on 12 March 1687. My father was a shoemaker; but I soon found myself aspiring towards some higher trade, and became apprenticed to a goldsmith. After several years I took the journeyman's examination. The work I submitted – such is the mockery of fate – was a ruby set in a golden shell. After two years of travelling, seeing the Alps, the ocean, and the spacious lands between them, I settled in Paris where I found a place with the goldsmith, Maître Lambert, in the rue Verdelet. His early death left me temporarily in charge of his workshop; and a year later I married his widow, thus attaining the rank of Master with full Guild rights. Over the next twenty years I succeeded in transforming the modest little establishment in the rue Verdelet into the largest and most respected jeweller's shop in the whole of Paris. My clients came from the city's most distinguished houses and from the best families in the land with Court connections. My rings, brooches, and diadems found their way into Holland, England, Germany. Many a crowned head crossed my threshold. In 1733, two years after the death of my beloved wife, I had the honour to be appointed Court Jeweller to the Duke of Orleans.

Admission into the most brilliant circles of our society was not without its effect on my intellectual development and the growth of my character.

I learned from the conversations to which I became accustomed, and from books to which I devoted my every spare minute. By such means, over the years, I acquired so fundamental an understanding of science, literature, and art that, although I had never attended a senior school or university, I could style myself without arrogance as a learned man. I mingled in all the leading salons, and received some of the most celebrated spirits of the age as my guests: Diderot, Dondillac, d'Alembert sat at my table. The correspondence I enjoyed for some years with Voltaire will be found among my posthumous papers. I counted even the retiring Rousseau among my friends.

I do not record these details with the aim of impressing my future reader – should he exist – with a roll-call of famous names. Rather do I seek to avoid reproaches when I come to reveal my unbelievable discoveries. It might be alleged that I am a poor fool whose claims are not be be taken seriously, coming from a scientific and philosophic ignoramus. I invoke those men as witnesses to the clarity of my intellect and my strength of judgment. To anyone who sees no reason to take me seriously, I have this to say: Who are you, my friend, to contradict a man whom the greatest of his time respected as an equal?

The enlargement of the workshop and extension of my business had made me a wealthy man. Yet, the older I became, the less enchantment gold and precious stones held for me, and the more I prized my books and scientific studies. And so, well before my sixtieth year, I resolved to withdraw from business life and pass my remaining days in prosperous retirement from the bustle of the capital. With this aim, I acquired a piece of land in the neighbourhood of Passy, where I had a spacious

house built together with a garden planted with a rich
variety of ornamental bushes, flower-beds, fruit trees, as
well as neat gravel paths and watery ways. The whole
retreat was separated from the outer world by a thick
boxtree hedge. In its alluring tranquillity it seemed a
fitting place for a man to enjoy a few years of peace and
pleasure between the cares of living and the moment of
death. On 22 May 1742, at the the age of fifty-five, I
moved from Paris to Passy and embarked on my new
existence.

Oh! When I think now of the happiness and quiet joy
of that spring day when I arrived at Passy. When I think
of the same night and of going to bed for the first time in
my life without the expectation of waking up to another
day of toil, delivery dates, rush and anxiety. With no
sound but the rustling of the alders in own garden, how
sweetly I slept – on the same cushion on which I now sit
like a stone. I do not know whether to curse or bless that
day. Since then, my path has been one of gradual self-
destruction, leading to my present wretched state. But
since then, too, the truth has been unveiled to me, piece
by piece; the truth of the beginning, the course, and the
end of our life, our world, and of our whole cosmos. The
face of truth is terrible, and its gaze as deadly as the Head
of Medusa. But, whether by accident or tireless searching, whoever finds the road towards it must pursue that
road to the end – even though this will bring him neither
peace nor comfort, nor any man's thanks.

At this point, my unknown reader, pause and examine
yourself before you read any further. Are you strong
enough to hear the worst of all? What I have to tell you
exceeds the outrageous, and when once I have opened
your eyes, you will see a new world and will no longer
see the old. The new world will be hateful. It will bring

oppression, distress, and torment. Stifle all expectation of any remaining hope, escape, or comfort – beyond the comfort that now you know the truth, and that the truth is final. Read no more if you fear the truth. Lay these pages aside if finality awakens your dread. Flee my words, if you cherish the peace of your soul. There is no shame in ignorance; to most of us it counts as happiness. It is, after all, the only possible happiness this world has to offer. Reflect before you throw it away!

What I now have to say to you is something you will never forget, for in your innermost heart you know it already – just as I knew it before it became obvious to me. We have only struggled against the impulse to acknowledge and express it: *The World*, I tell you, *is a shell that mercilessly closes-in on itself.*

Are you resisting me? Are you trying to defend yourself against that insight? No wonder. It is too big a step. One cannot make it all at once. The fog of ages is too thick to be dispersed by one great stroke of light. Instead we need a hundred little lamps. So I will resume the story of my life, and in this way you may gradually come to share in the enlightenment that befell me.

I have already described the garden that surrounded my new home. In reality, it was a small park, containing a multitude of rare flowers, shrubs, and trees. But, above all, I had it planted with simple roses, as the sight of a blossoming rose has always made a calming and comforting impression on me. I had given my gardener a free hand in matters of detail, and the good man, meaning to please me, had laid out a wide border of roses on the west-facing side of the house. He could not have guessed that, however much I liked looking at roses, I had no liking for them in rampant proliferation. Even less could he have guessed that the laying out of that flower-bed marked the beginning of a new and final chapter in the history of the human race. As for the roses, nothing could make them thrive. Their stems remained wretchedly small, many withering despite the most industrious watering, and while the rest of the garden came splendidly into bloom, the roses outside my western windows hardly put out a single bud. I discussed this with the gardener, whose only advice was to dig up the whole bed, and replant it with fresh soil. This struck me as a cumbersome solution, and as I was privately none too happy at having the roses so near to the house, I decided to uproot the whole border, and replace it with a terrace adjoining my salon, from which one might enjoy a view of the whole garden and admire the beauties of the sunset. I was so taken with this idea that I resolved to execute it myself.

I began by removing the rose trees and turning the earth, so that it could then be filled with gravel and sand as an underlay for paving stones. But after a few spade strokes I found I was no longer digging up loose earth. Instead I struck against a tough whitish stratum that made digging much harder. I took a pick-axe as a help to loosening it. It crumbled under the blows and broke up into small pieces which I dug up and put to one side. My specialist interest in this unfamiliar rock was reduced by the irritation of extra work, until my gaze fell on the loaded shovel I was about to empty. I saw a fist-sized stone, and a finely shaped object which seemed to be glued to its side. I put the spade down and took the stone in my hand, realising with amazement that this shapely object on the side of the stone was a petrified shell. At this point, I stopped work and went into the house to investigate my find. The shell appeared to have grown fixedly into the stone, and was hardly to be distinguished from it even by colour, as it shared the same pattern of white, yellow, and grey, which alternately deepened and splayed out like a fan, emphasising the raised grain. It was the size of a *louis d'or*, and its exterior was identical to the shells you find on the beaches of Normandy and Brittany, which form a popular lunch dish. When I took a knife and scraped the shell so as to break its surface, I found that there was no difference between that scratch and a scratch anywhere on the stone itself. I ground the broken-off piece of shell in one mortar and a piece of stone in another; both produced the same greyish-white powder. When mixed with a few drops of water, it resembled the paint used for whitewashing walls. The shell and the stone both consisted of one and the same substance. At first I did not fully grasp the monstrous implications of this finding. I was too taken by what I supposed to be a unique discovery, believing it to be an accidental whim of nature. It was beyond me to imagine anything else. But I soon had cause to change my mind.

After giving my shell a thorough examination, I returned to the rose-bed to see if there were any more to be found. I did not have to search for long. With every stroke of the pick-axe, with every lift of the spade, another shell came to light. Now that I knew what I was looking for, I found shells everywhere, where previously I had only seen stones and sand. In half an hour I collected over a hundred, after which I stopped counting. I would have needed more eyes to see them all.

Full of growing foreboding, even though, dear reader, I dared not acknowledge it, I went to the far end of the garden and began to dig there, too. To start with I found only earth and lime. But half a metre down I struck the shell-stones. I dug in a third and fourth, a fifth and sixth place. Everywhere – sometimes at the first stroke of the spade, sometimes at greater depth – I found shells, shell-stones, and shell-sand.

During the following weeks, I made excursions into the surrounding area. First I dug in Passy, then in Boulogne and Versailles, until finally I had systematically dug my way through the whole of Paris from St Cloud to Vincennes, from Gentilly to Montmorency, without once failing in my search for shells. Even when there were no shells, I found sand or stones which were materially identical. Along the course of the Seine and the Marne, the shells lay in profusion on the gravel banks; while at Charenton – where my labours were watched suspiciously by a guard from the local lunatic asylum – I had to dig a shaft to the depth of five metres before I made a strike. From every dig, I brought a few specimen shells and samples of the surrounding rocks back to my house, where I conscientiously examined them. In every case, the result of this research was exactly the same as with that of my first shell. The various shells in my collection exhibited no differences whatever, even in size; and, except for their shape, no difference from the stones to which they cleaved. This conclusion to my investigations and excursions prompted two fundamental questions, to which I both feared and longed to find the answer.

First: How far do the shells extend under the ground?

And secondly: How and why do the shells originate? Or, in other words, what causes an amorphous piece of stone – something of entirely arbitrary shape – to take on the elaborate form of a shell?

Reader, you may be inclined to interrupt me here to point out that such questions have already been discussed long ago by the great Aristotle, and that the occurrence of shell-stone is neither an original nor a surprising discovery; rather a phenomenon that has been familiar for a thousand years. To which I can only reply: Not so fast, my friend, not so fast!

I am far from claiming to be the first man to have found a petrified shell. Anyone with an eye for nature will have seen them. But no one has devoted so much thought and logical reflection to them as I have. Naturally I am familiar with the writings of the Greek philosophers concerning the origins of our planet, the continents and landscape, etc., which have a bearing on the discovery of petrified shells. After I had concluded the practical side of my research, I placed a Paris order for every book that might cast any light on the shell problem. I trawled through texts on cosmology, minerology, geology, astronomy and all related subjects. I read authors who had anything to say about shells from Aristotle to Albertus Magnus, from Theophrastus to Grosseteste, and from Avicenna to Leonardo.

What emerged from this was that while these mighty intellects exhibited ample knowledge of the incidence of shells and their appearance, structure, and distribution, when it came to their origin, their inner being, and the real purpose of their existence, these writers had nothing to say.

After my study of the texts, I at any rate could answer the question of how far shells had taken over the Earth. On the principle that there is no need to sail round the world to ascertain that that sky is blue, I had already arrived at the assumption that shells appear wherever you dig a hole to look for them. I read not only of shell finds in Europe and the breadths of Asia from the highest peaks to the deepest river valleys, but also of shell-lime, shell-sand, shell-stones, and cultivated shells which were to be detected in the newly discovered continents of North and South America. All this confirmed what I had feared from my reading of the Paris texts: namely that our whole planet has been undermined by shells and their cognate substances. That what we perceive as the real world – meadows and woodland, lakes and seas, gardens, fields, barren land and fertile plains – all this amounts to no more than a pleasing but insubstantial cloak over an obdurate core. If this thin cloak were removed, our planet would be seen as a grey-white ball, assembled and developed from myriad of petrified shells, each the size of a *louis d'or*. On such a planet, no life could survive.

One might dismiss the discovery that the world consists essentially of shells as a trivial curiosity, if it referred to a stable, unaltering state of affairs. Unfortunately, this is not the case. My exhaustive studies, which impending mortality prevents me from describing in detail, revealed that the petrification of the world is a rapidly advancing and unstoppable process. In our own time the earthly cloak is showing signs of fragility and fracture on all sides. In many places it is already chewed up and eaten away. Thus, we learn from the ancient authors that the island of Sicily, the North Coast of Africa, and the Iberian peninsula ranked as the most blessedly fertile in the antique world. Today, as everyone knows, these same regions consist – with a few exceptions – of dust, sand, and stones, which represent the preliminary stage of shell formation. The same applies to most of Arabia and North Africa; and, according to the latest reports, to previously unexplored areas of America. And even in our own country, which we generally view as a land of particular excellence, there is proof of the same incessant process. Thus, in Western Provence and the South Cevennes, the cloak has been reduced to the thickness of a finger. Altogether the surface of the globe that has already fallen victim to petrification considerably exceeds the area of Europe.

The cause for the inexorable spread of shells and shell substances lies in the inexorable circulation of water. For, just as the ocean supplies living shells with their normal habitat, so water proves to be the closest ally, indeed the native element of shell-stones. As every educated person knows, water describes an endless cycle in which, through the rays of the sun, it is drawn up from the sea and gathers itself into clouds which are then carried by the wind to fall as raindrops on the land. There it fills and pervades the earth down to the smallest particle, until, converging in springs and rivulets, it swells into brooks and rivers and so makes its way back to the sea. Water makes its most fatal contribution to the spread of shells at the stage where it penetrates the earth. Through saturation, the earth is gradually dispersed, broken up, and washed away. The water then seeps down until it reaches the shell stratum where, enriched with what it has absorbed from the soil, it delivers the nourishment necessary for the shells' development. In this way, the earth's surface is forever thinning while the shell-layer continues its ceaseless growth. Anyone can confirm my discovery by boiling water from a well in a saucepan. A whiteish deposit will form on the base and sides of the pan. And in pans that are repeatedly put to this use, the deposit develops to a considerable thickness. If one breaks off the crust and grinds it in a mortar, it yields the same powder that results from shell-stones. On the other hand, if one makes the same experiment with rainwater it produces no deposit.

My unknown reader will by now have grasped the desperate situation facing the world: that water, without

which we could not survive for a single day, destroys the
basis of our existence, the earth, and acts as the ally of our
deadly enemy, the shell. Thus the transformation of the
earth's life-giving elements into the stony instruments of
our destruction occurs as inescapably and irresistibly as the
metamorphosis of nature's blossoming variety into the
unvaried form of a shell. Let us entertain no more false
notions about the end of the world. It is as certain as sunrise
and sunset, as rising clouds and falling rain, that we will end
in total petrification. I shall describe this process in detail
on a later page. Before that, I must meet the objections that
will be raised against me, and which I understand all too
well. No man wants to acknowledge the worst, and fear
devises a thousand ifs and buts. It is the duty only of the
philosopher to take truth alone as his guide.

But, as I have already indicated, how miserably our
revered philosophers have failed when it comes to
explaining the shell phenomenon. Many of them make
light of it, and maintain it to be no more than an
accidental freak of nature; which, for some reason or
other, has imprinted stones with the form of shells. To
any intelligent person, this superficially consoling explanation – much promulgated to this day by Italian
authors – will appear so absurdly unscientific that I can
spare myself the trouble of discussing it.

A second view, which deserves to be taken more
seriously (as it has been by great philosophers), maintains
that in prehistory the ocean covered the entire world, and
that when it retreated the living shells were left behind. As
proof of this assertion, every scholar relies on the biblical
account of the Flood, where indeed it is stated as fact that
the whole earth up to its highest peaks was covered by
water. However illuminating this interpretation may seem
to the uninitiated, I must energetically contest it from my

informed vantage point. We read in the Book of Moses that the world was submerged for a total of three hundred and seventy days, and that the mountain peaks – where there were as many shells as on the plains – were covered for just a hundred and fifty days. How, I enquire, could a flood of such brief duration succeed in stranding such huge numbers as we find today? And in any case, the antediluvian shells of many thousand years must long before have been ground down and turned to sand by the weather. Even if, by some inexplicable means, they had been preserved, that still fails to account for the proven fact of their continuing increase. It thus emerges that every interpretation and explanation of the nature of shells, apart from my own, is baseless.

So far we have seen that the surface of our planet is subject to a continuous conversion from its manifold materials into the substance of shells. This bring us closer to the assumption that petrification represents a general principle governing not only the earth itself but all earthly life, every thing and being in the world, and indeed in the entire cosmos.

One look through a telescope convinced me long ago that our closest neighbour in the universe, the moon, offers a virtually classical example of cosmological petrification. Indeed, it has already reached the stage now facing the earth: namely the fully completed conversion of all materials into shell-substance. Admittedly there are astronomers, even Court astronomers, who declare the moon to be a congenial planet, with wooded hills, gentle meadows, great lakes and oceans. It has nothing of the kind. What these dilettantes mistake for oceans are vast shell-deserts, and what they designate as mountain ranges on their lunar maps are desolate heaps of shell-stones. The same applies to other heavenly bodies.

Later generations with sharper minds and more powerful telescopes will confirm that I am right.

Even more horrifying than the petrification of the cosmos is the constant decline of our own bodies into shell-substance. The process is so violent that in every case it leads inevitably to death. While at conception the human foetus only consists, if I may so express it, of a clot of slime, small but still quite free of shell-substance, it accumulates deposits during its growth in the womb. At birth, these are still quite soft and supple, as one may see from the heads of new-born babies. But within a short space of time, the bones and brain of the little body develop a hard stony cap, so that the child takes on a somewhat rigid posture. This pleases the parents, as it makes him seem a proper little man. They do not comprehend that it marks the onset of petrification, and that hardly has the little boy begun running than he is staggering towards his certain end. Admittedly, he enjoys an enviable condition compared to that of an old man. Among the old one may truly witness the full effect of human petrification: the skin hardens, the hair snaps, arteries, heart and brain calcify, the back buckles; taking on the structure of a shell, the man's whole figure bends and curves and finally topples into the grave as a wretched heap of stony rubble. Even that is not the end. For then the rain falls, its drops soak through the earth, and the water gnaws and dismembers him into minute fragments which it then flushes down to the shell stratum where, in the familiar form of shell-stones, he achieves his final rest.

Should anyone dismiss this picture as a fantasy, or accuse me of making unverified assertions, I can only ask him: Have you not observed the ossification of your own body, from year to year; how your movement has stiffened, and you have withered in body and soul. Have you forgotten how you used to jump, twist and bend when you were a child; falling and leaping up ten times a day as if there were nothing to it? Don't you remember your delicate skin, and the invincible vitality of your supple but powerful flesh? Look at yourself now! Your skin shrivelled into folds and wrinkles, your face carved into a scowl and twisted by aches and pains, your body stiff and creaking, every movement an effort, every step a decision; and always the tormenting fear of falling over and smashing into pieces like a brittle clay jug. Don't you feel it? Don't you feel the shell in every fibre of your body? Don't you feel it reaching towards your heart? Your heart is already half in its embrace. Whoever denies that is lying!

I myself present the greatest and saddest example of a man destroyed by shells. Although for years I have drunk rainwater, so as to minimise the growth of shell-substance, I of all people have suffered the most devastating attack. When I began writing this bequest a few days ago I still had the free use of my left hand. In the meantime the fingers have petrified to the extent that I can no longer lay the pen down without assistance. As speech causes me acute pain which absolutely forbids dictation, I am now compelled to write from the wrist with accompanying pushing and pulling motions of the whole arm. My exceptionally rapid petrification is no accident. I have occupied myself with shells for so long, and wrested so many secrets from them, that they have singled me out among all other men for a particularly cruel end. For although they face no threat to their power, they are in danger of losing their secret, which they guard with revengeful pride.

You may be surprised, unknown reader, to hear me speaking of these apparently lifeless stone-like things as beings capable of relating to a particular man and seeking vengeance on him. I shall therefore initiate you into the final and most appalling secret of the shell-water, by which you run the manifest danger of meeting a fate like mine.

From the very beginning of my experience of shells, I had wondered why a stone consisting of shell material should then go on to assume the invariable form of a shell. As usual, the philosophers who have tried to answer this all-important question leave us in the lurch. The only discussion of a *vis lapidificativa* comes from the Arab writer Avicenna, but even he can tell us nothing of the source of this power nor why it expresses itself in this manner. I, on the other hand, soon became convinced that behind the universal process of petrification there stood not only some unspecified power, but a directly animating force acting in obedience to a single higher Will. But, convinced as I was of its existence – having recognised its emanation through the fossilised shells – it was beyond me to imagine the being from which this Will derived. What kind of a being can one picture, that is set on stifling the human race, making a desert of the world, and transforming heaven and earth into an ocean of stone?

I meditated for a full year. I locked myself away in my study and racked my brains. I went back to nature in the hope of finding inspiration. All in vain. Finally, I have to confess that I found myself imploring this accursed unknown being for some sign of recognition. But nothing happened. My thoughts revolved in the same old tracks and life followed its old tormenting course: I was beginning to think that poor Mussard would go down to the shells, as far as the rest of mankind from understanding the final truth.

But then something amazing happened. I must describe it, and yet I cannot describe it, for it occupies a sphere, so to speak, that lies above and beyond the sphere of words. I will try to explain the inexplicable and to describe the indescribable, in their effect on me. Whether I make myself understood depends not least on you, my unknown reader, who have followed me thus far. I know that you will understand me if you have the will to do so.

It happened on an early summer day a year ago. The weather was lovely and the garden was in full bloom. The scent of roses accompanied me on my walk, and the birds sang as though trying to convince the whole world that they were immortal, and that this was not one of their last summers before the coming of the shells. It was about midday in the blazing sun. I sat down to rest on the bench, half in the shadow of an apple tree. In the distance I heard the splashing of the fountain. I felt tired and closed my eyes. Suddenly the sound of the fountain seemed to grow louder until it swelled into a roar. Then it happened. I was carried away from my garden and out into darkness. I had no idea of where I might be. I was surrounded by a darkness filled with unearthly gurglings and roaring, together with sounds of crunching and grinding. It seemed to me at that moment, if I dare so express it, that these two groups of sounds – the roaring waters and the crunch of stone – were those of the creation of the world. I was afraid. And at the height of my fear, I began falling through the darkness until the sounds grew distant and I emerged into blinding light. I continued falling through the light, away from the dark place which I now perceived as a monstrous mass of blackness. The further I fell, the more I could see of its vast extent; and at last I recognised the black mass as a shell. It then split into two parts, opening its black wings like some gigantic bird, until they covered the whole universe, and descended over me, over the world and everything that exists, over the light, and closed together in an eternal night, leaving only the pandemonium of roaring and crunching.

The gardener found me lying on the gravel path. I had tried to get up from the bench and collapsed from exhaustion. I was carried into the house and put into bed, never to get up again. I was so enfeebled that the doctor feared for my life. Not for three weeks did I make a partial recovery. What remains from that day is a clenching pain in my stomach, which intensifies day by day and steadily extends itself through the rest of my body. This is the shell disease, which has made an exemplary case of me, marking me out from the rest of humanity as the man who has seen the Shell. I have a bitter price to pay for my enlightenment, but I pay it gladly, as I alone know the answer to the final question: the power that holds all life in its spell and drives everything to its end, the high Will that controls the universe and condemns it to petrification as proof of its own omni-presence and omnipotence, all this stems from the great First Shell from whose inner depths I have briefly been released so as to behold its magnitude and terrible majesty. What I saw was a vision of the end of the world. When the petrification of the world has advanced to the stage where mankind is compelled to acknowledge the power of the Shell; when men, exposed in their impotence and terror, cry aloud to their gods for help and deliverance, the only answer of the Great Shell will be to open its wings and close them over the world, and grind everything into itself.

Now that I have told you everything, my unknown reader, what is there left to say? How can I comfort you? Should I drivel on like the philosophers and prophets about the immortality of the soul, the grace of a merciful God, the resurrection of the body? Should I pass the Shell off as a gracious divinity; or ape the cults of Yahveh and Allah by proclaiming human salvation through a cult of the Shell? What purpose would that serve? Why should I lie? It has been said that man cannot live without hope. That never saved anyone from dying. My concern, as I feel I shall not survive until tomorrow, is not to begin lying on my last night on earth. It is a relief finally to be coming to the end of my dying. You, my poor friend, are still in the midst of it.

Afterword by Claude Manet,
servant to Maître Mussard

Today, 30 August 1753, at the age of sixty-six, my good master, Maître Mussard, died. I found him early in the morning, sitting in bed in his usual position. I was unable to close his eyes as their lids could not be moved. When I tried to take the pen from his hand, my master's left index-finger snapped like glass. The corpse-washer had hard work in dressing him, as his body would not relinquish its rigid sitting posture after the onset of rigor mortis. Dr Procope, my master's friend and physician, could only advise us to order a right-angled coffin. So, on the first day of September, the horrified mourners at the Passy cemetery witnessed a right-angled grave, in which my master was showered with a thousand roses and consigned to his last rest. May God take mercy on his soul.

Translated by Irving Wardle

Faith
Joanna Trollope

When my mother died, she left me a bookstore. In England, you would call it a bookshop, but I prefer the word store. It suggests a treasure house to me, a place full of riches and surprises. 'Shop' is more pedestrian. A shop is for the purchase of kettles and bacon and birdseed.

My mother's bookstore is in a town some two hours' drive east of Seattle and a hundred miles south of the Canadian border. It was settled by Scandinavians in the last century and if it has a domestic symbol, it must be the coffee pot. The whole town is crazy about coffee, addicted to it. There is a coffee shop, one of a national chain, opposite my mother's bookstore, and all day long people run in and out of it for pints and quarts of coffee in giant Styrofoam cups, carrying them back to their automobiles and places of work with a kind of tender greed.

Because we are so close to the Canadian border, and so far west, Alaskans come down to our town in the winter in search of warmth and work. A lot of them end up sleeping rough or in the beaten-up taxis they ply without a proper licence. Sometimes I find them sleeping in the bookstore doorway, and I give them money to go and buy coffee in the shop across the street. I'm sorry for them, but I don't want them in my doorway. The other immigrants are Asians from the Pacific Rim, mostly Vietnamese, who inhabit a danger-

ous and feuding underworld. They slip through our
town on their way between Seattle and Spokane, eluding
gang vendetta. Neither they, nor the drug-mazed
Alaskans, have any use in the world for a bookstore
specialising in English literature.

Although she never said so directly, I believe my
mother opened her bookstore to console herself for
disappointment in marriage. She was English and not
of a generation to abandon a bad marriage and in any
case, my grandmother had been a Catholic and a pious
woman and had instilled into my mother that vows were
vows. My grandmother died when my mother was
twenty, and left her daughter in the care of her father,
a good-natured, romantic man who managed a small
theatre in Yorkshire, a pretty little theatre built in the
time of the English Regency. My grandfather had no
religion, my mother said, but he had dreams. Once, I
knew, his dreams had got him into serious trouble, but of
that my mother would say nothing.

Sometimes I wonder if I have taken after him. I am
not a religious woman in any way but I have noticed that
I have sometimes given way to dreams. My most intense
dream was when I was twenty-four, and contemplating
going to Boston to work in a distinguished publishing
house, and I fell in love with a man in our town. He was
married, with three children, and I had known him all
my life, and I fell in love with a violence that quite
terrified me. We had an affair, all one summer; I shall
never forget it. And then quite suddenly he told me it
was impossible, it was over, he was leaving. He collected
up his wife and his children and, in the exaggerated way
of people in this vast country of ours, took off across
seven states to Greensboro, North Carolina, where he
vanished, like a stone thrown into a pool. I still cannot

look at the daily weather charts on television with any
equanimity when the weather girl's hand sweeps over
the southeastern states.

My mother took me back in, after the death of that
dream. She made me a bedroom in the apartment above
the store, and she gave me customers to look after and
shelves to dust and arrange. My father, by then, was
living in a two-room condo on the edge of Elliott Bay, in
Seattle. My mother had bought the condo, and settled
him there, along with his typewriter and his wardrobe of
lumberjack shirts and his eloquent, empty declarations of
one day being a renowned novelist, a chronicler of his
time and the American Northwest. It was those declarations that had once made my mother fall in love with
him. And I believe that it was those same declarations,
after twenty years of talk and drink and quarter-finished
manuscripts, that finally set her teeth on edge.

My mother determined to make a bookstore unlike
any bookstore she had known in her English childhood.
They were stiff, hushed places, she said, where one
whispered as if in church, and was not allowed to touch
books without specific intention of purchase. My
mother's bookstore was in a converted dance studio –
Latin American tangos were once taught there to combat
the effect of our low grey winter skies – and she divided
the space up with bookshelves to make a series of little
rooms, and put armchairs about with worn cretonne
covers, and reading lamps, and made a play area for
children with toys on a rug and a rocking horse. She
made friends of her customers; she encouraged them to
read. They brought photographs of their grandchildren
to show her, and batches of cookies and problems.
Sometimes, I must admit, I was jealous of her customers.

She also had festivals in the store. At Hallowe'en she

filled the window with pumpkins and witches' hats and at the New Year, she dressed it up for Scottish Hogmanay with antlers and tartan ribbons. None of that I minded; indeed, I applauded her enterprise. But at Easter, and at Christmas, I cringed. I pleaded with her every year not to give way to cheap sentiment, to superstition, but she took no notice, she went ahead. Year after year, twice a year, I had to endure the spectacle, in this remarkable store that was a shrine to the glory of the English language, of a holy garden at Easter and a crib at Christmas.

My mother made the garden herself every year, with mosses and spring flowers, and a cave built of stones collected on Sunday walks in the woods. The crib she had bought on her honeymoon in southern France, in Provence. It was made of some kind of pottery clay, easily chipped and crudely painted. She set it up in the children's corner between two candles, in a ruff of ivy, and it caused me, her own and only child, mortification of the acutest kind.

When she died, I felt I had two choices. Either I allowed the bookstore to remain exactly the same, a shrine to her memory, or I made some changes. I decided upon the latter. I am a better businesswoman than my mother, and although I have inherited her love of literature, I am not alarmed by technology as she was, nor opposed to the commercial sense of stocking business and computer books. I cleaned up the store a little. I took away most of the armchairs because too many people had become accustomed to lunching in them and I did not want my stock spoiled by smears of tuna mayonnaise. I changed my mother's sentimental festivals into book-orientated festivals to celebrate a prizewinning novel, a major biography, a breakthrough

cookbook. I held business-book seminars at lunchtime
and poetry readings at night. I started a gift-wrapping
service and opened discount accounts for local schools
and companies.

My mother's customers told me the store had lost its
heart. I refrained from telling them that it was no longer
losing money. My grief for my mother might make me
resentful at any implied criticism of my treatment of her
memory, but it wasn't going to make me forget my
manners. The store was not as full as it had been when
my mother was alive – sometimes it had resembled a
bridal shower in noise and atmosphere – but I had three
times the number of account customers, most of them
institutions. I had to hire a boy to help with the packing.

At night, when I had finally closed the store and set
the new security alarm, I would go up to the apartment
above and drink a single glass of wine. Merlot was my
choice usually; sometimes I drank a Cabernet Sauvignon.
When I had drunk my wine, I fixed myself something
quick to eat in the microwave, and then I would settle
down with a mug of coffee – Costa Rica, medium roast
– to my mother's papers. It was an indulgence, a nightly
fix as cherished as the glass of Merlot.

It took me almost a year and a half to get through
everything my mother left – diaries, letters, photographs,
playbills, cuttings, reviews, notes and quotations
scribbled on the backs of envelopes.

'I can't tell you everything that's happened to me,' my
mother said before she died. 'I've forgotten the half of it.
But you will find everything you want to know. It's all
there.'

I read everything. I am a methodical person, and I
discarded nothing before reading it. I made scrapbooks
and collections of letters in labelled boxes. I put pictures

into chronological order and slid them into the vinyl pockets of albums. I copied quotations into a common-place book, and made a history of the founding of the bookstore in a green boxfile. I hoped it would be a therapy for me, but it was the reverse. Every night I longed to find something that would reconcile me to my mother's passing, and every night she rose before me, more vivid than ever, and I missed her wretchedly. I even felt – and I am aware this is unjust – that she, with her English heritage and English assumptions, had left me stranded here alone in a country which was my birth-place but to which, because of her, I could never quite belong.

I also felt estranged by her Catholic upbringing. There were several rosaries in her drawers, and a couple of prayer books, and above her bed had always hung a reproduction of a Della Robbia Madonna and Child, a blue-and-white porcelain plaque. I left all these things where I found them, but I would have preferred them out of the way. Just as I would have preferred my mother – so intelligent, so warm and witty, who scarcely in my lifetime even entered a church – not to have clung so blindly to these leftover trappings of a child's past. It sometimes seemed to me like a dreadful falseness in a person otherwise so transparently honest. But we didn't talk about it. It was the only thing we didn't talk about. She said that there was no point, because she could see that my mind was made up.

Early last December, we had some terrible rains. It wasn't cold, but it was wild and wet and windy and the weather kept customers away. A businessman, whom I supplied with computer books, said that I should consider re-locating to the new shopping mall outside our town where there was all-weather parking. I told

him I would then suffer from the proximity of a big
chain bookstore, offering immense discounts, and he
gave me a considering look and I could see he knew
about the immense discounts already, and was turning his
loyalty to me over in his mind.

When he had gone, I closed the store early and went
upstairs to my apartment. It was not time yet for my ritual
glass of Merlot, so instead I obeyed my mother's lifelong
habit and made a pot of loose-leaf Lapsang Souchong tea.
I took this with me into my living room and put on the
lamps and pulled the drapes against the wet black
evening. Only one drawer of my mother's papers
remained to me, and I was dreading its being sorted.

It lay on the rug in front of the electric fire my mother
had insisted upon as reminding her of England. I put my
tea down on the floor and then I knelt down and lifted
out a heap of assorted envelopes in which mail had come
over the years and which my mother thriftily hoarded.
One of them was large and bulky. It had come from
Hatchards, the English bookstore in Piccadilly, London,
and had probably contained a catalogue. Now it had a
white gummed label stuck across it, not quite straight, on
which my mother had written in her bold hand 'About
my father'.

I untucked the flap of the envelope and held it open
over my hearthrug. A shower of papers fell out, news-
paper cuttings mostly, and a memo badly typed on sheets
of thin white paper held together with a rusting clip. I
unfolded some of the cuttings. They were from English
newspapers, some provincial, some national, and there
were disturbing headlines: 'Theatre Manager's Theft';
'Manager Defrauds Theatre'; 'Hand in the Box Office
Till'. I picked up the memo. I could see at once from the
way it was typed that it had been typed by my mother. It

had no heading, only a date – November 1956. In 1956 I was twelve, and my mother's bookstore was only two years old. By 1956 my English grandfather had been a widower for sixteen years.

I quickly saw that the memo had not merely been typed by my mother, but written by her, too. She described my grandfather, so wedded to his theatre that he was there seven days a week, and six nights a week, too, dressed in a black evening suit with a stiff-fronted white shirt and a black bow tie, welcoming theatregoers into the foyer. She described herself, too, going to the theatre as a child with her father and standing on the empty stage listening to the seats tipping up in the empty auditorium as the temperature changed, as if a ghostly audience waited in perpetuity for the show to begin.

She said my grandfather did everything in that theatre. It belonged to the Town Council, who furnished a board of trustees like characters from an Arnold Bennett novel, bluff, uncompromising, respectable northern citizens. Once a month, my grandfather reported to the board of trustees and wrestled with their lack of imagination, their deep-seated philistinism. In the early spring of 1956, after thirty-five years of unremitting labour for the theatre, my grandfather asked for a few months' leave of absence. He gave the trustees to understand that he would be visiting his daughter and granddaughter in America. The trustees, much startled, eventually agreed, as long as he took it upon himself to find a temporary manager.

My grandfather did find a manager, but he did not come to America. Instead, he went in search of a place that my mother said had been the dream passion of his life; he went, alone, to look for the seat of King Arthur, for the site of Camelot.

It took him three months. He went from Caerleon upon Usk to Winchester, and from thence to Cadbury Camp near Queen Camel in Somerset and to Tintagel in the Camel county of Cornwall. He hired a good automobile and stayed in good hotels. He kept a comprehensive and scholarly journal which he bequeathed at his death to a northern university to assist those studying the legends of King Arthur and the works of the poet Tennyson. And while he was away the temporary manager discovered – with no difficulty since my grandfather had scarcely troubled to conceal it – that the funds used to pay for this comfortable and chimerical journey had been removed from the straitened coffers of the theatre.

My grandfather was summoned before the trustees. He was perfectly open. He had no defence beyond this longing that had built up to a craving to find the place that had so seized upon his mind. He was perfectly happy to repay the funds by working for no more than a pittance until the debt was cleared. He then stood and looked at those solid, practical northern faces, and waited for certain dismissal and probable arrest.

'And did you,' one trustee asked, 'find Camelot?'

My grandfather admitted that he had failed.

'Then we may assume that you no longer believe in the possibility of its existence?'

My grandfather was deeply shocked. 'Oh no,' he said, in gentle reproof, 'I believe as I ever did.'

The trustees let him keep his job. 'It was the only moment,' my mother wrote, 'in all his dealings with them, when he felt that their minds were in tune with his.'

I put the memo down and merely sat there on my living-room floor. My tea had grown quite cold. I sat there for perhaps half an hour and then I rose, rather stiffly, and went into the little room my mother had always called the box room, in her English way, where we kept the lumber of our lives. I hunted about among the bundles and bales until I found the cardboard box containing the little crib figures from Provence, and I carried it down to the darkened and empty store.

There was just enough light coming in from the street to illumine what I wanted to do. I cleared a space in the window in the display of Christmas cookery books I had arranged among ivy trails and decorative pyramids of clementines and walnuts, and in it I set out the Virgin Mary in her blue robe and Joseph in his brown one and the baby in his bed of stiffly painted straw. I added the shepherds to one side and the clumsy ox and ass to the other, and positioned the three Magi at a discreet distance to await the coming of Twelfth Night. Then I fetched from my kitchen one of the slow-burning nightlights my mother had liked by her bed during the last weeks of her life, and lit it, and put it below the figures in a small green saucer. It threw a pool of faint light over the central figures and cast their shadows up against the books behind them. I stood and looked at the scene for a few moments, and then I went back upstairs to pour myself a glass of wine. I am not, as I have said, a religious woman and I never will be. But I knew then – and will now know for ever – the curious power of possibility.

Two Boys and a Girl
Tobias Wolff

Gilbert saw her first. This was in late June, at a party. She was sitting alone in the back yard, stretched out on a lawn chair, when he went to get a beer from the cooler. He tried to think of something to say to her but she seemed complete in her solitude and he was afraid of sounding intrusive and obvious. Later he saw her again, inside – a pale, dark-haired girl with dark eyes and lipstick smears on her teeth. She was dancing with Gilbert's best friend, Rafe. The night after that she was with Rafe when he picked Gilbert up to go to another party, and again the night after that. Her name was Mary Ann.

Mary Ann, Rafe, and Gilbert. They went everywhere together that summer, to parties and movies and the lake, to the pools of friends, and on long aimless drives after Gilbert got off work at his father's bookstore. Gilbert didn't have a car, so Rafe did the driving; his grandfather had given him his immaculate old Buick convertible as a reward for getting into Yale. Mary Ann leaned against him with her bare white feet up on the dash while Gilbert sprawled like a pasha in the back and handed out the beers and made ironic comment on whatever attracted his notice.

Gilbert was very ironic. At the high school where he and Rafe had been classmates, the yearbook editors voted him 'most cynical'. That pleased him. Gilbert believed disillusionment to be the natural consequence, even the duty, of a mind that could cut through the authorised version to the true nature of things. He made it his business to take nothing on trust, to respect no authority but that of his own judgment, and to be elegantly unsurprised at the grossest crimes and follies, especially those of the world's anointed.

Mary Ann listened to what he said, even when she seemed to be occupied with Rafe. Gilbert knew this, and he knew when he'd managed to shock her. She clenched her hands, blinked rapidly, and a red splotch, vivid as a birthmark, appeared on the milky skin of her neck. It wasn't hard to shock Mary Ann. Her father, a captain in the Coast Guard, was the squarest human being Gilbert had ever met. One night when he and Rafe were waiting for Mary Ann, Captain McCoy stared at Gilbert's sandals and asked what he thought about the beatniks. Mrs McCoy had doilies all over the house, and pictures of kittens and the Holy Land and dogs playing poker, and in the toilets these chemical gizmos that turned the water blue. Whenever Gilbert took a leak at Mary Ann's house he felt sorry for her.

In August Rafe went fishing in Canada with his father. He left Gilbert the keys to the Buick and told him to take care of Mary Ann. Gilbert recognised this as what the hero of a war movie says to his drab sidekick before leaving on the big mission.

Rafe delivered his instructions while he was in his room packing for the trip. Gilbert lounged on the bed watching him. He wanted to talk but Rafe was playing his six-record set of *I Pagliacci*, which Gilbert didn't believe he really liked, though Rafe made occasional humming noises as if he knew the whole score by heart. Gilbert thought he was taking up opera the same way he'd taken up squash that winter, as an accessory. He lay back and was silent. Rafe went about his business: he was graceful and precise, and he assembled his gear without waste of motion or any hesitation as to where things were. At one point he walked over to the mirror and studied himself as if he were alone, and Gilbert was surprised by the anger he felt. Then Rafe turned to him and tossed the keys on the bed and spoke his line about taking care of Mary Ann.

The next day Gilbert drove the Buick around town all by himself. He double-parked in front of Nordstrom's with the top down and smoked cigarettes and watched the women come out as if he were waiting for one of them. Now and then he examined his watch and frowned. He drove on to a pier at the wharf and waved at one of the passengers on the boat to Victoria. She was looking down at the water and didn't see him until she raised her eyes as the boat was backing out of the slip and caught him blowing a kiss at her. She stepped away from the rail and vanished from sight. Later he went to La Luna, a bar near the university where he knew he wouldn't get carded, and took a seat from which he could see the Buick. When the bar filled up he walked outside and raised the hood and checked the oil, right in front of La Luna's big picture window. To a couple walking past he said, 'This damn thing drinks oil like it's going out of style.' Then he drove off with the expression of a man with important and not entirely pleasant business to perform. He stopped and bought cigarettes in two different drugstores. He called home from the second drugstore and told his mother he wouldn't be in for dinner and asked if he'd gotten any mail. No, his mother said, nothing. Gilbert ate at a drive-in and cruised for a while and then went up to the

lookout above Alki Point and sat on the hood of the
Buick and smoked in a moody, philosophical way,
deliberately ignoring the girls with their dates in the
cars around him. A heavy mist stole in from the sound.
Across the water the lights of the city blurred, and a
foghorn began to call. Gilbert flipped his cigarette into
the shadows and rubbed his bare arms. When he got
home he called Mary Ann, and it was agreed that they
would go to a movie the following night.

After the movie Gilbert drove Mary Ann back to her
house, but instead of getting out of the car she sat where
she was and they went on talking. It was easy, easier than
he had imagined. When Rafe was with them Gilbert
could speak through him to Mary Ann and be witty or
deep or outrageous. But in the moments they'd been
alone, waiting for Rafe to rejoin them, he had always
found himself tongue-tied, in a kind of panic. He'd
cudgel his brains for something to say, and whatever he
did come up with sounded tense and sharp. But that
didn't happen, not that night.

It was raining hard. When Gilbert saw that Mary Ann
wasn't in any hurry to get out, he cut the engine and they
sat there in the faint marine light of the radio-tuning
band with liquid shadows playing over their faces from
the rain streaming down the windows. The rain
drummed in gusts on the canvas roof but inside it was
warm and close, like a tent during a storm. Mary Ann
was talking about nursing school, about her fear that she
wouldn't measure up in the tough courses, especially
Anatomy and Physiology. Gilbert thought she was being
ritually humble and said, Oh, come on, you'll do fine.

I don't know, she said. I just don't know. And then
she told him how badly she'd done in Science and

Maths, and how two of her teachers had personally gone down to the nursing-school admissions office to help her get in. Gilbert saw that she really was afraid of failing, and that she had reason to be afraid. Now that she'd said so herself, it made sense to him that she struggled in school. She wasn't quick that way; wasn't clever. There was a simplicity about her.

She leaned back into the corner, watching the rain. She looked sad. Gilbert thought of touching her cheek with the back of his hand to reassure her. He waited a moment, then told her it wasn't exactly true that he was trying to make up his mind whether to go to the University of Washington or Amherst. He should have corrected that misunderstanding before. The actual truth was, he hadn't gotten into Amherst. He'd made it on to the waiting list, but with only three weeks left until school began he figured his odds were just about nil.

She turned and regarded him. He couldn't see her eyes. They were dark pools with only a glint of light at the bottom. She asked why he hadn't gotten in.

To this question Gilbert had no end of answers. He thought of new ones every day, and he was sick of them all. I stopped working, he said. I just completely slacked off.

But you should have gotten in wherever you wanted. You're smart enough.

I talk a pretty good game, I guess. He took out a cigarette and tapped the end against the steering wheel. I don't know why I smoke these damn things, he said.

You like the way they make you look. Intellectual.

I guess. He lit it.

She watched him closely as he took the first drag. Let me, she said. Just a puff.

Their fingers touched when he handed her the cigarette.

You're going to be a great nurse, he said.

She took a puff of the cigarette and blew the smoke out slowly.

Neither of them spoke for a time.

I'd better go in, she said.

Gilbert watched her go up the walkway to her house. She didn't hunch and run but moved sedately through the lashing rain as if this were a night like any other. He waited until he saw her step inside, then turned the radio back up and drove away. He kept tasting her lipstick on the cigarette.

When he called from work the next day her mother answered and asked him to wait. Mary Ann was out of breath when she came to the phone. She said she'd been outside on a ladder, helping her dad paint the house. What are you up to? she asked.

I was just wondering what you were doing, he said.

He took her to La Luna that night, and the next. Both times they got the same booth, right near the jukebox. 'Don't Think Twice, It's Alright' had just come out and Mary Ann played it again and again while they talked. On the third night some guys in baseball uniforms were sitting there when they came in. Gilbert was annoyed and saw that she was, too. They sat at the bar for a time but kept getting jostled by the drinkers behind them. They decided to go someplace else. Gilbert was paying his tab when the baseball players stood up to leave, and Mary Ann slipped into the booth just ahead of an older couple who'd been waiting nearby.

We were here first, the woman said to Mary Ann as Gilbert sat down across from her.

This is our booth, Mary Ann said, in a friendly, informative way.

How do you figure that?

Mary Ann looked at the woman as if she'd asked a truly eccentric question. Well, I don't know, she said. It just is.

Afterwards it kept coming back to Gilbert, the way Mary Ann had said 'our booth'. He collected such observations and pondered them when he was away from her: her breathlessness when she came to the phone, the habit she'd formed of taking puffs from his cigarettes and helping herself to his change to play the jukebox, the way she listened to him, with such open credulity that he found it impossible to brag or make excuses or say things merely for effect. He couldn't be facetious with Mary Ann, she always thought he meant exactly what he said, and then he had to stop and try to explain that he'd actually meant something else. His irony began to sound weak and somehow envious. It sounded thin and unmanly.

Mary Ann gave him no occasion for it. She took him seriously. She wrote down the names of the books he spoke of – *On the Road*, *The Stranger*, *The Fountainhead*, and some others that he hadn't actually read but knew about and intended to read as soon as he found the time. She listened when he explained what was wrong with Barry Goldwater and *Reader's Digest* and the television shows she liked, and agreed that he was probably right. In the solemnity of her attention he heard himself saying things he had said to no one else, confessing hopes so implausible he had barely confessed them to himself. He was often surprised by his own honesty. But he stopped short of telling Mary Ann what was most on his mind, and what he believed she already knew, because of the chance that she didn't know or wasn't ready to admit she did. Once he said it, everything would change, for all of them, and he wasn't prepared to risk this.

They went out every night but two, once when
Gilbert had to work overtime and once when Captain
McCoy took Mary Ann and her mother to dinner. They
saw a couple more movies and went to a party and to La
Luna and drove around the city. The nights were warm
and clear and Gilbert put the top down and poked along
in the right lane. He used to wonder, with some
impatience, why Rafe drove so slowly. Now he knew.
To command the wheel of an open car with a girl on the
seat beside you was to be established in a condition that
only a fool would hasten to end. He drove slowly around
the lake and downtown and up to the lookouts and then
back to Mary Ann's house. The first few nights they sat
in the car. After that, Mary Ann invited Gilbert inside.

He talked; she talked. She talked about her little sister,
Kathleen, who had died of cystic fibrosis two years
before, and whose long hard dying had brought her
family close and given her the idea of becoming a nurse.
She talked about friends from school and the nuns who
had taught her. She talked about her parents and grand-
parents and Rafe. All her talk was of her affections.
Unconditional enthusiasm generally had a wearying
effect on Gilbert, but not on these nights with Mary
Ann. She gave praise, it seemed to him, not to shine it
back on herself or to dissemble some secret bitterness but
because that was her nature. That was how she was, and
he liked her for it, as he liked it that she didn't question
everything but trusted freely, like a child.

She had been teaching herself the guitar and sometimes she would consent to play and sing for him, old
ballads about mine disasters and nice lads getting hanged
for poaching and noblewomen drowning their babies.
He could see how the words moved her: so much that
her voice would give out for moments at a time, during

which she would bite her lower lip and gaze down at the floor. She put folk songs on the record player and listened to them with her eyes closed. She also liked Roy Orbison and the Fleetwoods and Ray Charles. One night she was bringing some fudge from the kitchen just as 'Born to Lose' came on. Gilbert stood and offered his hand with a dandified flourish that she could have laughed off if she'd chosen to. She put the plate down and took his hand and they began to dance, stiffly at first, from a distance, then easily and close. They fitted perfectly. Perfectly. He felt the rub of her hips and thighs, the heat of her skin. Her warm hand tightened in his. He breathed in the scent of lavender water with the sunny smell of her hair and the faint salt smell of her body. He breathed it all in again and again. And then he felt himself grow hard and rise against her, so that she had to know, she just had to know, and he waited for her to move away. But she did not move away. She pressed close to him until the song ended, and for a moment or two after. Then she stepped back and let go of Gilbert's hand and in a hoarse voice asked him if he wanted some fudge. She was facing him but managing not to look at him.

Maybe later, he said, and held out his hand again. May I have the honour?

She walked over to the couch and sat down. I'm so clumsy.

No you're not. You're a great dancer.

She shook her head.

He sat down in the chair across from her. She still wouldn't look at him. She put her hands together and stared at them.

Then she said, How come Rafe's dad picks on him all the time?

I don't know. There isn't any particular reason. Bad chemistry, I guess.

It's like he can't do anything right. His dad won't let him alone, even when I'm there. I bet he's having a miserable time.

It was true that neither Rafe's father nor his mother could take any pleasure in their son. Gilbert had no idea why this should be so. But it was a strange subject to have boiled up out of nowhere like this, and for her to be suddenly close to tears about. Don't worry about Rafe, he said. Rafe can take care of himself.

The grandfather clock chimed the Westminster Bells, then struck twelve times. The clock had been made to go with the living-room ensemble and its tone, tinny and untrue, set Gilbert on edge. The whole house set him on edge: the pictures, the matching Colonial furniture, the single bookshelf full of condensed books. It was like a house Russian spies would practise being Americans in.

It's just so unfair, Mary Ann said. Rafe is so sweet.

He's a good egg, Rafe, Gilbert said. Most assuredly. One of the best.

He is the best.

Gilbert got up to leave and Mary Ann did look at him then, with something like alarm. She stood and followed him outside, on to the porch. When he looked back from the end of the walkway she was watching him with her arms crossed over her chest. Call me tomorrow, she said. OK?

I was thinking of doing some reading, he said. Then he said, I'll see. I'll see how things go.

The next night they went bowling. This was Mary Ann's idea. She was a good bowler and frankly out to win. Whenever she got a strike she threw her head back and gave a great bark of triumph. She questioned Gilbert's score-keeping until he got rattled and told her to take over, which she did without even a show of protest. When she guttered her ball she claimed she'd slipped on a wet spot and insisted on bowling that frame again. He didn't let her, he understood that she would despise him if he did, but her shamelessness somehow made him happier than he'd been all day.

As he pulled up to her house Mary Ann said, Next time I'll give you some pointers. You could be half decent if you knew what you were doing.

He heard that 'next time'. He killed the engine and turned and looked at her. Mary Ann, he said.

He had never said so much before.

She looked straight ahead and didn't answer. Then she said, I'm thirsty. You want a glass of juice or something? Before Gilbert could say anything, she added, We'll have to sit outside, OK? I think we woke up my dad last night.

Gilbert waited on the steps while Mary Ann went into the house. Paint cans and brushes were arranged on top of the porch railing. Captain McCoy scraped and painted one side of the house every year. This year he was doing the front. That was just like him, to eke it out one side at a time. Gilbert had once helped the Captain make crushed ice for drinks. The way the Captain did it, he held a single cube in his hand and clobbered it with a hammer until it was pulverised. Then another cube. Then another. Etcetera. When Gilbert wrapped a whole tray's worth in a hand towel and started to bang it on the counter the Captain grabbed the towel away from him. That's not how you do it! he said. He found Gilbert another hammer and the two of them stood there hitting cube after cube.

Mary Ann came out with two glasses of orange juice. She sat beside Gilbert and they drank and looked out at the Buick gleaming under the streetlight.

I'm off tomorrow, Gilbert said. You want to go for a drive?

Gee, I wish I could. I promised my dad I'd paint the fence.

We'll paint, then.

That's all right. It's your day off. You should do something.

Painting's something.

Something you like, dummy.

I like to paint. In fact I love to paint.

Gilbert.

No kidding, I love to paint. Ask my folks. Every free minute, I'm out there with a brush.

Like fun.

So what time do we start? Look, it's only been three hours since I did my last fence and already my hand's starting to shake.

Stop it! I don't know. Whenever. After breakfast.

He finished his juice and rolled the glass between his hands. Mary Ann.

He felt her hesitate. Yes?

He kept rolling the glass. What do your folks think about us going out so much?

They don't mind. I think they're glad, actually.

I'm not exactly their type.

Hah. You can say that again.

What're they so glad about, then?

You're not Rafe.

What, they don't like Rafe?

Oh, they like him, a lot. A whole lot. They're always saying how if they had a son, and so on. But my dad thinks we're getting too serious.

Ah. Too serious. So I'm comic relief.

Don't say that.

I'm not comic relief?

No.

Gilbert put his elbows on the step behind him. He looked up at the sky and said, carefully, He'll be back in a couple of days.

I know.

Then what?

She leaned forward and stared into the yard as if she'd heard a sound.

He waited for a time, aware of every breath he took. Then what? he said again.

I don't know. Maybe . . . I don't know. I'm really kind of tired. You're coming tomorrow, right?

If that's what you want.

You said you were coming tomorrow.

Only if you want me to.

I want you to.

OK. Sure. Tomorrow, then.

Gilbert stopped at a diner on the way home. He ate a piece of apple pie, then drank coffee and watched the cars go past. To an ordinary person driving by he supposed he must look pretty tragic, sitting here alone over a coffee cup, cigarette smoke curling past his face. And the strange thing was, that person would be right. He was about to betray his best friend. He was about to cut Rafe off from the two people he trusted most, possibly, he understood, from trust itself. Himself, too, he would betray – his belief, held deep under the stream of his flippancy, that he was steadfast and loyal. And he knew what he was doing. That was why this whole thing was tragic, because he knew what he was doing and could not do otherwise.

He had thought it all out. He could give himself reasons. Rafe and Mary Ann would have broken up anyway, sooner or later. Rafe was moving on. He didn't know it, but he was leaving them behind. He'd have roommates, guys from rich families who'd invite him home for vacation, take him skiing, sailing. He'd wear a tuxedo to debutante parties where he'd meet girls from Smith and Mt. Holyoke, philosophy majors, English majors, girls with ideas who were reading the same books he was reading and other books, too, who could say things he wouldn't have expected them to say. He'd get interested in one of these girls and go on road trips with his friends to her college. She'd come to New Haven. They'd rendezvous in Boston, New York. He'd meet her parents. And on the first day of his next trip home, honourable Rafe would enter Mary Ann's house and leave half an hour later with a sorrowful face and a heart leaping with joy. There wouldn't be many more trips home, not after that. What was here to bring him all that way? Not his parents, those crocodiles. Not Mary Ann. Himself? Good old Gilbert? Please.

And Mary Ann, what about Mary Ann? When Rafe double-timed her and then dropped her cold, what would happen to that simple goodheartedness of hers? Would she begin to suspect it, stand guard over it? He was right to do anything to keep that from happening.

These were the reasons, and they were good reasons, but Gilbert could not make use of them. He knew that he would do what he was going to do even if Rafe stayed at home and went to college with him, or if Mary Ann was somewhat more calculating. Reasons always came with a purpose, to give the appearance of struggle between principle and desire. But there'd been no

struggle. Principle had power only until you found what
you had to have.

Captain McCoy was helping Mrs McCoy into the car
when Gilbert pulled up behind him. The Captain waited
as his wife gathered her dress inside, then closed the door
and walked back toward the Buick. Gilbert came around
to meet him.

Mary Ann tells me you're going to help with the
fence.

Yes, sir.

There's not that much of it – shouldn't take too long.

They both looked at the fence, about sixty feet of
white pickets that ran along the sidewalk. Mary Ann
came out on the porch and mimed the word Hi.

Captain McCoy said, Would you mind picking up the
paint? It's that Glidden store down on California. Just
give 'em my name. He opened his car door, then looked
at the fence again. Scrape her good. That's the secret.
Give her a good scraping and the rest'll go easy. And try
not to get any paint on the grass.

Mary Ann came through the gate and waved as her
parents drove off. She said that they were going over to
Bremerton to see her grandmother. Well, she said. You
want some coffee or something?

I'm fine.

He followed her up the walk. She had on cut-offs.
Her legs were very white and they flexed in a certain
way as she climbed the porch steps. Captain McCoy
had set out two scrapers and two brushes on the railing,
all four of them exactly parallel. Mary Ann handed
Gilbert a scraper and they went back to the fence. What
a day! she said. Isn't it the most beautiful day? She knelt
to the right of the gate and began to scrape. Then she

looked back at Gilbert watching her and said, Why don't you do that side over there? We'll see who gets done first.

There wasn't much to scrape, some blisters, a few peeling patches here and there. This fence is in good shape, Gilbert said. How come you're painting it?

It goes with the front. When we paint the front, we always paint the fence.

It doesn't need it. All it needs is some retouching.

I guess. Dad wanted us to paint it, though. He always paints it when he paints the front.

Gilbert stopped, looked behind him at the gleaming white house, the bright weedless lawn trimmed to the nap of a crewcut.

Guess who called this morning, Mary Ann said.

Who?

Rafe! There was a big storm coming in so they left early. He'll be back tonight. He sounded really great. He said to say hi.

Gilbert ran the scraper up and down a picket.

It was so good to hear his voice, Mary Ann said. I wish you'd been here to talk to him.

A kid went by on a bicycle, cards snapping against the spokes.

We should do something, Mary Ann said. Surprise him. Maybe we could take the car over to the house, be waiting out front when he gets back. Wouldn't that be great?

I wouldn't have any way to get home.

Rafe can give you a ride.

Gilbert sat back and watched Mary Ann. She was halfway down her section of the fence. He waited for her to turn and face him. Instead she bent over to work at a spot near the ground. Her hair fell forward, exposing the nape of her neck. Maybe you could invite someone along, Mary Ann said.

Invite someone. What do you mean, a girl?

Sure. It would be nice if you had a girl. It would be perfect.

Gilbert threw the scraper against the fence. He saw Mary Ann freeze. It would *not* be perfect, he said. When she still didn't turn around he stood and went up the walk and through the house to the kitchen. He paced back and forth. He went to the sink, drank a glass of water, and stood with his hands on the counter. He saw what Mary Ann was thinking of, the two of them sitting in the open car, herself jumping out as Rafe pulled up, the wild embrace. Rafe unshaven, reeking of smoke and nature, a little abashed at all this emotion in front of his father but pleased, too, and amused. And all the while Gilbert looking coolly on, hands in his pockets, ready to say the sly mocking words that would tell Rafe that all was as before. That was how she saw it going. As if nothing had happened.

Mary Ann had just about finished her section when Gilbert came back outside. I'll go get the paint, he told her. I don't think there's much left to scrape on my side, but you can take a look.

She stood and tried to smile. Thank you, she said.

He saw that she had been in tears, and this did not soften him but confirmed him in his purpose.

Mary Ann had already spread out the tarp, pulling one edge under the fence so the drips wouldn't fall on the grass. When Gilbert opened the can she laughed and said, Look! They gave you the wrong colour.

No, that's exactly the right colour.

But it's *red*. We need white. Like it is now.

You don't want to use white, Mary Ann. Believe me.

She frowned.

Red is the perfect colour for this. No offence, but white is the worst choice you could make.

But the house is white.

Exactly, Gilbert said. So are the houses next door. You put a white fence here, what you end up with is complete boredom. It's like being in a hospital, you know what I mean?

I don't know. I guess it is a lot of white.

What the red will do, the red will give some contrast and pick up the bricks in the walk. It's just what you want here.

Well, maybe. The thing is, I don't think I should. Not this time. Next time, maybe, if my dad wants to.

Look. Mary Ann. What your dad wants is for you to use your own head.

Mary Ann squinted at the fence.

He said, You have to trust me on this, OK?

She sucked in her lower lip, then nodded. OK. If you're sure.

Gilbert dipped his brush. The world's bland enough already, right? Everyone's always talking about the banality of evil — what about the evil of banality?

They painted through the morning and into the afternoon. Every now and then Mary Ann would back off a few steps and take in what they'd done. At first she kept her thoughts to herself. The more they painted, the more she had to say. Toward the end she went out into the street and stood there with her hands on her hips. It's interesting, isn't it? Really different. I see what you mean about picking up the bricks. It's pretty red, though.

It's perfect.
Think my dad'll like it?
Your dad? He'll be crazy about it.
Think so? Gilbert? Really?
Wait till you see his face.